JOSSEY-BASS™
A Wiley Brand

Profitable Raffles & Auctions

72 Ways to Boost Your Revenue

Scott C. Stevenson, Editor

WILEY

978-1-118-69147-2   ISBN

978-1-118-70427-1   ISBN (online)

Profitable Raffles and Auctions
72 Ways to Boost Your Revenue

Published by
Stevenson, Inc.
P.O. Box 4528 • Sioux City, Iowa • 51104
Phone 712.239.3010 • Fax 712.239.2166
www.stevensoninc.com

Profitable Raffles and Auctions

Table of Contents

Profitable Raffles and Auctions

Table of Contents

Profitable Raffles and Auctions

1. A Variety of Raffles

The type of raffle you select will depend on: a) whom you hope to attract, b) how much you hope to raise and c) what you intend to give away.

There are many types of raffles. Here are brief descriptions of popular ones:

1. **Grand Prize Raffle.** This is a great option for a stand-alone raffle event. But, unless you get the grand prize donated, you may have to pay for all or part of the prize. Your ticket price will be set higher as well. Consider giving away smaller secondary prizes along with the grand prize so your buyers have a greater chance of winning.

2. **Chinese Raffle.** Instead of giving guests the opportunity to win random prizes, guests apply their tickets to prizes they'd like to win. Have the prizes on-site with ticket holders in front of each prize. This is great for events where the raffle is a secondary event.

3. **50/50 Split Raffle.** The grand prize is the money from the ticket sales. The winner splits their winnings (e.g., 50/50, 75/25, 60/40, etc.) with your organization. You can vary the numbers however you chose. This raffle gives you the option of not buying or getting prizes donated.

4. **Calcutta Raffle.** This is a raffle within a raffle. Guests bid on and buy "lots" of numbers that may hold the winning raffle ticket. They're buying the chance of having the same numbers as the winning ticket. The guest with the winning lot wins the entire cash bid, usually split with the organization. The greater the odds of choosing the winning lots, the greater the amount of bid money. Be sure to check the legality of this in your state/city.

2. Add Online Component to Your Next Fundraising Auction

When preparing for your next live or silent auction event, consider adding a new component to increase auction sales: an online auction.

The advantage to adding this online option is that it allows those who support your cause and/or have interest in the items up for bid but are unable to attend the opportunity to bid. This, in turn, can result in significantly higher final bids and a better overall result for your auction-driven event.

To generate additional interest in your auction, offer items online that will not be available at the live and/or silent auction portion of the event. This will serve to significantly increase your earnings potential and may get online bidders to also attend your special event.

3. Auction Tracker Software

Looking for a way to manage your live or silent auction? Auction-Tracker™ software from Northwest Software Technologies, Inc. allows you to track donors, guests and auction items; produce a catalog; and even provide receipts for the IRS. It makes checkout quick and easy.

Also available are A'Thon Tracker™ for sponsor-based pledge events, Banquet Tracker™ and Tournament Tracker™.

For more info: Visit www.nwsoftware.com

4. Hospital Launches Multi-year, Multi-million-dollar Raffle

When it comes to special events, don't be afraid to dream big, like organizers of a mega raffle who hope to sell 110,000 tickets and give away thousands of prizes.

"The Phoenix Children's Hospital (Phoenix, AZ) Raffle offers more than 15,000 extraordinary prizes, including a grand prize of up to seven $1 million cash prizes, vehicles with gas cards, dream vacations and a variety of innovative home electronics," says Debra Stevens, director of marketing and communications.

Major Raffle Is Years in Planning

Hospital and foundation representatives spent two years preparing for this major raffle with assistance from Winning Charities (Brockville, Ontario, Canada), a consulting firm with experience in large hospital raffles. They researched raffle vendors, conducted primary research, made presentations to foundation and hospital operating boards, and developed and launched operational and marketing plans. "There is certainly risk in launching an endeavor of this magnitude," Stevens says. "That's why we spent so much time in the research and planning phase. Thus, we were able to minimize risk and launch the program with strong confidence in its success."

Multi-faceted PR Campaign Helps Spread Word, Sell Raffle Tickets

One challenge tackled in the research and planning stage was the development of a comprehensive marketing plan crucial to the raffle's success.

"Because Winning Charities has experience in managing children's hospital raffles, they have a comprehensive template plan and existing vendor relationships. Of course, that template was customized for this market," Stevens says. "On the hospital and foundation staff, three people were directly involved in marketing decisions. Beyond that, marketing elements were planned and executed by Bill Bayles of Winning Charities, with assistance from three marketing vendors," a direct mail specialist Bayles had worked with previously, plus two Phoenix agencies.

While marketing plan details are confidential, Stevens says it includes print, radio and broadcast ads, billboards, direct mail, e-marketing, direct sales and public relations. Additionally, Stevens participated in approximately 25 media interviews.

Local TV Station Invites Raffle Representative for Multiple Appearances

"Publicity opportunities have been excellent," she says. "It's been a great chance to tell the story of the hospital and how the hospital will be improved."

For instance, the local ABC affiliate aired a 30-minute show taped at the hospital in which Stevens promoted the raffle and highlighted the hospital's unique programs, doctors, patients and an expansion project. TV station officials invited Stevens to be a morning show guest nine times throughout the duration of the raffle, giving her opportunity to showcase the hospital while promoting the raffle.

Organizers hope the raffle will help to raise between $5 million and $10 million over three to five years to enhance patient care.

"While the Phoenix Children's Hospital Raffle is not an inexpensive venture, it is self-financing," Stevens says. "The program was thoroughly researched and planned, and costs are being carefully managed so that we maximize the return."

Source: Debra Stevens, Director of Marketing and Communications, Phoenix Children's Hospital, Phoenix, AZ. Phone (602) 546-1000.
E-mail: dstevens@phoenixchildrens.com

Raffle Gives Many Chances to Win

It's a raffle of massive proportions: Staff and supporters of Phoenix Children's Hospital (Phoenix, AZ) aim to sell 110,000 tickets and give away more than 15,000 prizes. Tickets are available in the hospital lobby, by phone, mail or online for $100 for one, $250 for three or $500 for seven.

Odds of winning are one in seven. Participants can win prizes in several drawings:

❑ **Early Bonus Draw:** Up to 25 persons each win a plasma TV.

❑ **Earlybird Draw:** One person will win a 2009 911 Carrera Cabriolet Porsche and a $10,000 gas card.

❑ **Travel, Minor Prize Draw:** Prizes include travel packages, home theatre systems, digital cameras and DVD players.

❑ **Grand Prize Draw, Grand Prize Playoff, Final Draw:** Seven finalists are drawn. Each selects an envelope that will determine their prize. One person will receive $1 million cash, a Cadillac Escalade and $5,000 gas card. Six each win a vehicle with the possibility of winning $1 million if the temperature hit 86 degrees Fahrenheit Feb. 14 at the Phoenix Sky Harbor Airport, says Debra Stevens, director of marketing and communications. For additional information, see related story, left.

5. Theatre Guild Brings Experience of Tony Awards to Life

Staff and supporters with the Theatre Guild at Proctors (Schenectady, NY) were looking for a way to raise funds with an exciting event that was the outgrowth of the love they had for Broadway Theater.

The result? Tony Night, a popular event since 2006.

With the opening of the expanded theater in 2007, guests now enjoy the unique experience of viewing the CBS Broadcast of the Tony Awards on a giant Iwerks movie screen, located inside of Proctors' own GE Theatre. The GE Theatre has retractable stadium seating that gives the planners the option of having attendees sit at tables instead of the usual theatre seating. As a result, guests are able to enjoy a fabulous, four-course dinner served at their table during the broadcast.

Judy Decker, events manager, says this popular special event really is all about guests experiencing the feeling of being celebrities for the special night. To that end, guests arrive on the red carpet, which leads to a champagne reception held in the atrium lobby outside of the theatre. Throughout the evening, guests are treated to live entertainment during the broadcast's commercial breaks and witness the honoring of local talent through the Proctors Regional Arts Awards.

Decker says guests are also able to participate in a "theatergoer's dream of a silent auction with performance tickets, artwork and celebrity items up for grabs. For example, auction bidders had the opportunity to bid on tickets to the American Theatre Wing's Tony Awards 2010 at Radio City Music Hall."

To add to the evening's fun, guests are given ballots, and can follow along, voting for their favorite Broadway performers.

In the end though, Decker says the most unique feature of the evening remains the venue. "Guests comment to us that seeing the Tony's on the huge screen makes them feel like they are among the celebrities. Making an event successful is really about bringing a unique event or experience to life for people."

The 120 people who attended Tony Night 2009 raised more than $14,000 through ticket sales, sponsorships and the silent auction.

Source: Judy Decker, Events Manager, Proctors, Schenectady, NY. Phone (518) 382-3884. E-mail: jdecker@proctors.org

6. Auction Item Getaways

Don't overlook unique locales for auction vacations and getaways.

Looking for imaginative getaways for your auction event? Turn to friends and businesses to line up a slew of donated getaway possibilities:

- A weekend on a houseboat
- Overnights at special bed and breakfasts
- A white-water rafting trip
- A week on a dude ranch
- A stay at a unique hotel (The Library Hotel, NY www.libraryhotel.com)
- A group stay at a Y or church camp
- A romantic night in a castle
- A week at an exclusive spa
- A scenic train ride
- A week at a real farm
- A fall foliage tour

7. Move Your Auction Online

The auction at your annual event is already a huge success. Why take it online?

Because doing so gives you access to countless more bidders, says Jon Carson, CEO, cMarket, Inc. and biddingforgood.com (Cambridge, MA).

"In today's soft economy, auction fundraisers need every edge they can get," says Carson. "A physical special event is already restricted by a variety of factors (e.g., geography, the economy, weather, etc.). The fewer people in attendance, the fewer bids placed on items and the fewer overall dollars raised for your cause."

Recent market surveys also indicate donors of auction items are looking for more marketing value to justify their donation, he adds.

Online auctions, Carson says, give donors more reach and measurable marketing value from their donations, which can lead to more item donations, which in turn, "makes it easier to attract more bidders from across the country 24/7."

An additional perk? The sell to board members may be easier than you think. The low cost of running an online auction and opportunity for increased bids can be appealing to those familiar with auction fundraising.

Carson's only caveat is items that require physical inspection, such as artwork or jewelry. With such items, he says, it's best to allow people to preview them at your event first, then kick off your online auction.

Source: Jon Carson, CEO, cMarket, Inc., Cambridge, MA. Phone (866) 621-0330. E-mail: biddingforgood@cmarket.com

8. Make Silent Auction Bidding Fair to All

Q: What are the etiquette rules for a silent auction? How do you enforce them so bidding is fair to all persons?

"One of our best rules in our annual silent auctions is our Buy It Now. We have normal increments to increase the value of the items, but we also have the last line say, 'Buy it Now.' The bidder can place his or her bidder number next to the 'Buy it Now' and pay 150 to 200 percent more than the fair market value but is guaranteed the item. It avoids a bidding war and eliminates hovering. I think it works really well. We get top dollar, plus if someone really wants the item, he or she can get it."

— Cindy Behnke, Manager of Promotions and Fundraising, Salem Christian Homes (Chino, CA)

"My staff and I have a few points to ensure good etiquette for a silent auction:
- ✓ Print bidding rules in the program and on silent-auction-table signage.
- ✓ Assign spotters to monitor the table. Make sure you have enough volunteers.
- ✓ Make sure there is no hovering over particular items. Keep the flow around auction tables moving.
- ✓ Make sure the pen and bid sheet are accessible for each item.
- ✓ Have minimum bid increment amounts posted on each auction item sheet.
- ✓ Post silent auction times including when it starts and when it will end.
- ✓ If possible, announce table closings frequently.
- ✓ Make sure assigned staff and spotters pick up bid sheets at the close of the auction as quickly as possible."

— Helen Snyder, Director of Development, The Hearing and Speech Agency (Baltimore, MD)

9. Designer Handbags Have Female Donors in Their Clutches

Looking for a fundraising event to introduce female donors to your cause? Consider a designer handbag auction and sale, such as these two events:

Content not available in this edition

Bag Ladies Luncheon for Make-A-Wish Foundation of Central and Western North Carolina (Charlotte, NC):

Selena Rogers, CEO, says bidding gets competitive at her organization's Bag Ladies Luncheon, which started in 2005. "It's fun to watch and good for the bottom line."

The event raised $30,000 from 300 attendees. Guests enjoy a champagne luncheon where they bid on designer handbags. Volunteers and chapter staff recruit sponsors, sell tickets and secure new and gently used handbags to be auctioned at the event. The event has been so successful, the Make-A-Wish Foundation is in the process of registering "Bag Ladies Luncheon" for a trademark.

Mama's Got a Brand New Bag Auction for S.A.F.E., Inc. (Tupelo, MS):

Maggie Atwood Caldwell and Rhonda Herring turned their passion for purses into this fundraiser benefiting a domestic abuse shelter. Some 300 ladies attended the first-time event, set up in office space adjacent to a city-wide festival, bidding on 40 designer purses. Winning bids averaged $40 and topped out at $300. This year's event will be a stand-alone Girls' Night Out at a local restaurant's rooftop venue, with hopes to double the amount raised the first year.

Sources: Maggie Atwood Caldwell, Organizer, Mama's Got a Brand New Bag, Tupelo, MS. Phone (662) 844-4466. E-mail: mcaldwell@dwc-associates.com
Selena Rogers, CEO, Make-A-Wish Foundation of Central and Western North Carolina, Charlotte, NC. Phone (704) 339-0334. E-mail: srogers@ncwish.org

---

Seven Ways to Make Your Handbag Auction a Success

Maggie Atwood Caldwell and Rhonda Herring, organizers of the Mama's Got a Brand New Bag fundraising event (Tupelo, MS), offer seven tips to make your designer purse/clutch/handbag sale or auction a success:

1. Group items in sections, with at least 30 minutes' difference in end times for each auction section. This keeps the evening flowing, streamlines the checkout process and gives time to build excitement and competition among bidders.

2. Require must-be-present-to-win and payment at the event. This will save you from having to track people down after the event.

3. Provide Buy-me-now items. Sell less-expensive makeup clutches filled with promotional items from sponsors (e.g., nail files, samples, coupons, gift certificates) for $5. In true grab-bag style, don't let buyers look inside until they pay.

4. Fill every purse with a brochure explaining who benefits from the purchase.

5. Pick an exclusive location. This year's Mama's Got a Brand New Bag event will be held at a restaurant with the city's only rooftop environment.

6. Appeal to environmentalists by encouraging recycling gently used bags by donating them to the auction, noting the tax deduction they get for doing so.

7. Offer a wide variety of bags to guarantee the auction appeals to many women.

10. New Twist to Gift Basket Fundraiser

Does your organization do a May Basket or other gift basket fundraiser that includes silent auction theme baskets filled with donated items? To raise even more from your basket-themed silent auction, include this offer on your invitation: "We will be taking orders for May Baskets (holiday baskets, etc.) through April 25 to be delivered to recipients on May 1."

Offer two types of baskets for delivery — one for children, one for adults. When invitees return auction RSVPs, they can also order basket deliveries.

11. Three Things to Look for in a Benefit Auctioneer

So you're considering hiring a professional auctioneer for your live auction. Where do you start? What makes a good benefit auctioneer? How do you find one?

Sean Kelly, The Charity Auctioneer (San Diego, CA), says ask these questions to help identify a good match for your cause:

1. How many auctions has the auctioneer done? How many benefit auctions does he/she do each month?

2. Does he/she belong to the National Auctioneer's Association (NAA)? This indicates how seriously he/she takes the profession. Also, NAA members are likely to engage in continuing education.

3. Has candidate attended the NAA's Benefit Auctioneer Specialist course? If so, he/she is considered a benefit auction expert.

What if the candidate has none of the above qualifications? Look for someone with a public speaking background.

"Stage presence is really important," says Kelly. "Do they know how to put smiles on people's faces in a conservative setting, without offending? Do they understand that raising money comes first, being funny a close second? It's not about them. It's about the organization raising as many funds as possible."

Avoid auctioneers who only auction cattle, cars, estates, real estate, etc., Kelly says. "A benefit auctioneer should be able to auction anything, but any auctioneer isn't a benefit auctioneer. The experience your supporters have at the auction will determine whether or not supporters will come back next year and the amount raised. If your auctioneer pushes too hard, you might just wind up losing your best supporters."

Source: Sean Kelly, The Charity Auctioneer, San Diego, CA. Phone (619) 757-4674. E-mail: funny.sean@gmail.com

---

Hiring a Professional Pays Off

Think you can't afford a professional auctioneer? Think again, says Sean Kelly, The Charity Auctioneer (San Diego, CA): "An auctioneer who has graduated from bid calling school and has been given training from a senior auctioneer will always raise far more money than a 'personality.'"

Along with calling the auction, most professional auctioneers provide additional services to help auctions succeed, including pre-auction consulting, assistance in securing auction items, recommendations for appropriate items based on your audience and possible referrals to public relations, marketing or other professionals who can improve the quality of your event.

For organizations with smaller budgets, Kelly says to have a senior benefit auctioneer match you with a newer professional auctioneer whose fee may be more within your budget.

Don't be afraid to be selective when choosing your event's auctioneer.

12. Red Shoe Ball Offers Dancing and Donations

Event organizers of the Red Shoe Ball – an annual fundraiser for the Ronald McDonald House (Missoula, MT), understand ruby red slippers are beloved by more than a small girl from Kansas lost in the Land of Oz.

Since 2007, volunteers and organizers of the ball have crafted a highly successful red-shoe-themed event that features dinner, dancing and a live auction. Proceeds from the ball, which takes place at Missoula's Hilton Garden Inn, go toward operating costs for the house.

Hand-crafted or one-of-a-kind items often draw significant interest at charity auctions.

Art Event Morphs Into Red Shoe Ball

The most recent event, held April 12, 2010, netted $35,000. Revenue sources included sponsorships, donations, auctions, raffle sales, ticket sales and registration costs.

"The first year for a ball benefiting Missoula's Ronald McDonald House was 2006," says Barbara Wickel, executive director of Missoula's Ronald McDonald House. "The event's theme was Art From the Heart and featured an art auction and the grand opening of Hilton Garden Inn. Hilton has been a major sponsor," she shares. "The event morphed into the Red Shoe Ball the second and third year," she says, explaining that the opportunity to forego black ties and wear red shoes has generated a good deal of interest.

Shoes, Sponsors and a Geek Squad Spell Success

"The event has been successful because of all of the energy and fun related to wearing red shoes — the shoes are a great conversation piece," Wickel says. "In addition, we have very little overhead and have minimal advertising. Our success is also the result of returning sponsors and very loyal patrons."

Wickel shares that the mechanics behind preparing the event included planning nine months in advance and involved 35 volunteers. Participants included specialty volunteers, area college fraternities and sororities, a volunteer auctioneer and a bank and accounting firm staff, who volunteer to run the registrations and check out. Wickel says Best Buy and The Geek Squad are major sponsors each year.

Adding a Hint of Handmade Mystery

"The last three years also featured theme items to bid on," Wickel says. "There were mystery suitcases, where donors were asked to pack a suitcase representing a mystery location. For instance, an England-themed suitcase may harbor China teacups, tea, a quilt, etc. Italy's themed suitcase might include pasta, a pottery-serving bowl, a travel book, etc. Guests could also bid on hand-painted and decorated children's chairs and hand crafted and donated lamps."

Wickel says that the handcrafted items proved to be a big enough hit to warrant their return for their next event on March 4, 2011. "People appreciate supporting these creative works," she says, as well as the opportunity to create their own favorite pair of red dancing shoes. "Women generally buy their shoes for the event, but men make theirs, often with spray paint, red duct tape, etc."

At a Glance —	
Event Type:	Live and silent art auction featuring dinner, dancing
Gross:	$50,000
Costs:	$15,000
Net Income:	$35,000
Volunteers:	35
Planning:	9 months
Attendees:	225
Revenue Sources:	Sponsorships, donations, raffle, auction, tables, dinner registrations ($75/ticket)
Unique Feature:	All attendees encouraged to wear red shoes.

Source: Barbara Wickel, Executive Director, Ronald McDonald House, Missoula, MT. Phone (406) 541-7646. E-mail: Barbara@rmhmissoula.org. Website: www.rmhmissoula.org

13. Branding, Varied Activities Ensure a Dazzling Event

The annual fundraiser of the Los Gatos Education Foundation (Los Gatos, CA) needed tweaking. While the event was raising money, the confusion attendees seemed to have about proper attire suggested problems with branding and messaging, says Kimberley Ellery, director of special events.

The solution? Denim and Diamonds.

"The theme really established the tone of the evening," Ellery says. "The décor was casual but elegant — red roses and crystal — and the guests looked fabulous. They were very comfortable in their jeans, but outstanding in their jewelry."

Organizers wove the diamond motif throughout the event, from promotional artwork to a jeweler selling diamonds (and donating a portion of the proceeds to the foundation) at the event itself.

While the theme got people in the door, Ellery credits the variety of activities for securing their support. "We were very deliberate about offering many levels of participation at different price points," says Ellery. "People could jump in for as little as $20, or offer thousands through family sponsorships."

The event's many activities included:

At a Glance —	
Event Type:	Themed Gala
Gross:	$135,000
Costs:	$45,000
Net Income:	$90,000
Volunteers:	6
Planning:	9-12 months
Attendees:	275
Revenue Sources:	Ticket sales, live and silent auctions, blackjack tables, poker tourney, jewelry sales, sponsorships, more
Unique Feature:	Wide variety of activities, price points

To keep guests excited and involved, make sure to incorporate a range of differing games, raffles and contests.

- **Chicken Bingo.** A fenced, 7X7-foot grid of 100 squares was brought to the dance floor and attendees bought individual squares for $20. A diamond-wearing chicken was then placed on the grid, and the owner of the square where it did its business won diamond earrings. Of the event, Ellery says, "You could have heard a pin drop in that room, everyone was so fascinated. It was a perfect way to focus attention for the auction."

- **Heads-or-tails Raffle.** For $30, participants called successive coin flips until only one remained, winning an iPad tablet computer.

- **Premium Wine Bar.** Guests paid $25 per glass to sample fine wine donated by local vineyards. Five-glass punch cards were available for $100.

- **Best of Raffle.** 100 tickets were sold at $100 each, with the winner receiving his or her choice of any single item offered in the live auction.

- **Wine Toss.** For $15 a toss, attendees attempted to ring the necks of donated bottles of wine. Those who succeeded won the wine and an auction item valued at $50 or less. Ellery says, "It's a great way to get rid of leftover bits that can't be easily packaged or auctioned off, packs of five carwash certificates and things like that."

Other activities including a ticketed Texas Hold 'Em tournament, black jack tables, and live and silent auctions helped the event net $90,000.

Source: Kimberley Ellery, Director of Special Events, Los Gatos Education Foundation, Los Gatos, CA. Phone (408) 402-5014. E-mail: KimberleyEllery@comcast.net

14. Try Something New With an Online Quilt Auction

Since Colonial times, American quilts have helped mark history. Quilts created for an online auction to benefit your cause can also mark history — time when your nonprofit organization utilized historic means to raise the funds necessary to support your cause.

Consider the following when implementing an online quilt auction:

❑ Determine if you will ask a local quilting group to create one quilt for online bidding or whether there are enough talented quilters in your area to place several quilts up for auction.

❑ Seek out local quilters and quilting clubs to find those willing to donate quilts for your cause. Serious quilters work consistently to create beautiful quilts and may have extras on hand.

❑ If a quilter or group will make a special quilt for the occasion, ask for a quilt that merges symbolically with your cause in color or design.

❑ Create a page on your website that features bidding options and outlines auction rules, as well as photos of quilts up for auction. Include information about the quilter/quilting group.

❑ Consider a starting bid requirement for all quilts so that the bidding does not begin unusually low.

❑ Make the extra effort to notify your more affluent donors, individually, of the unique fundraising opportunity and welcome their bids.

❑ Promote your quilt auction throughout your community as you would any other fundraising event. Place ads and promote the event heavily at your website as well as in your newsletter.

❑ Clearly display the hours that you will accept bids on your website, and watch the activity begin!

Offer unusual auctions as an opportunity to reach out to enthusiasts, hobbyists and suppliers who are unfamiliar with your organization.

15. Champagne Raffle Puts New Twist on Chamber Event

A champagne raffle proved popular with attendees of the annual luncheon-fashion show hosted by the Hoffman Estates Chamber of Commerce (Hoffman Estates, IL).

Every $10 raffle ticket sold for the chance to win a $915 necklace came with a free glass of regular or non-alcoholic champagne, says Cheri Sisson, chamber president.

The raffle cost very little, thanks to the generosity of the hotel owner who donated the champagne and a local jeweler who donated the necklace. Both were billed as major sponsors, receiving name recognition in chamber newsletters, advertising efforts, flyers and event programs. The jeweler also received the chamber's annual President Award.

The champagne raffle contributed $600 to the event's $10,000 proceeds. The proceeds are used for the chamber's operating costs and an annual scholarship fund.

Source: Cheri Sisson, President, Hoffman Estates Chamber of Commerce, Hoffman Estates, IL. Phone (847) 781-9100. E-mail: info@hechamber.com

16. **Auction Off Business Connections**

Pulling off a successful fundraising auction is a challenge when the economy is down, as normally impulsive bidders may hesitate about spending the cash, especially for frivolous items.

Enter the auction of a valuable commodity: business leads.

The Michigan Council of Women in Technology (MCWT) of Auburn Hills, MI, raises up to $30,000 in a single event by auctioning off time with Michigan-based chief information officers at large corporations such as GM, GMAC, Ford, Lear Corporation and Comerica Bank.

"We've auctioned them off primarily to companies who want to do business with them — technology vendors like Compuware, Oracle, IBM, Information Builders and CSC," says Kathleen Norton-Schock, vice president of marketing at the council dedicated to increasing the number of women working in technological fields.

They auction the opportunities at two annual fundraisers — a golf outing and black-tie fundraiser. At the golf outing, bidders vie for the chance to play golf with company representatives. At the black-tie event, they bid to have dinner with them.

"We have more than 500 attendees, a number of whom work for information technology or telecommunications vendors or consultants — Microsoft, IBM, Oracle, Sun Microsystems — highly motivated to have lunch or dinner with a targeted CIO at a company with whom they already do business or want to do business," she says. "So we inform them via e-mailed newsletters a month ahead of time who will be up for auction. They internally strategize to decide on whom they want to bid."

Source: Kathleen Norton-Schock, Vice President of Marketing, Michigan Council of Women in Technology, Auburn Hills, MI. Phone (248) 335-4445. E-mail: knorton-schock@ardentcause.org

17. **Seek Auction Donations of Items Combined With Service**

As you seek donations for your silent and/or live auction, look to donors who can offer both a donation and a service. These examples will help make the point:

✓ An Alaskan salmon dinner for eight with fish provided by someone just back from an Alaskan fishing trip.

✓ A hundred square feet of patio brick donated and installed by a professional stone mason.

✓ A website design created by an ad agency, independent graphic designer, corporation's webmaster or college/technical school student.

✓ A hog roast for 12 with meat provided by a local farmer and prepared by someone experienced at doing so.

✓ Full car detailing — including seat and carpet shampoo — provided by a local car dealership.

✓ Installation of a pond, stream or other water feature, complete with landscaping, by a local landscaping firm.

✓ Creation of a wedding or prom dress by a professional seamstress.

✓ A new set of golf clubs along with a session with a golf pro to help the winning bidder develop a winning swing.

18. Brassiere Fashion Show & Auction Turns Heads, Raises Funds

Brainstorming for a unique way to raise funds for the CarePartners Hospice Foundation and for the Hope Chest fund of Hope Women's Cancer Centers, event organizers tapped into an attention-getting idea — a brassiere fashion show and auction.

Classy Bras for Sassy Broads featured a Brassieres on Parade Auction in which women volunteers from the community, ages 16 to 54, modeled bras, halters, corsets and other tops created by area artists and designers. Organizers say the event was tastefully done while still turning heads and gaining attention community-wide.

Consider holding a pre-event preview party to build anticipation for the bidding that will follow.

The event drew nearly 150 guests at $35 each, raising $5,600 from ticket sales and live and silent auction items that complemented the theme of pampering women including spa packages, jewelry and gift bags. The local Hooters restaurant sponsored the event, with two of its employees greeting guests at the door.

Content not available in this edition

Kristie Quinn, event coordinator and planner, shares tips she learned through the new event:

❑ Draw people with an eye-popping invitation. Organizers of the Classy Bras for Sassy Broads event worked closely with a trusted graphic design company to create the stunning invitation above.

❑ When setting a deadline for creative submissions, realize that artists and designers tend to work up to the deadline and typically work well under deadline pressure. Schedule buffer time in to your event schedule to allow for this aspect of working with a creative team.

❑ With a fashion show auction as the main event, communicate clearly with guests on how bidding works. Allow ample bidding time.

❑ Have designers invite guests to the show. Whether those guests are interested bidders or just there to support the artist, friends and family of that artist should cheer and express their enthusiasm to energize the crowd while the artist's piece is on the runway.

❑ When obtaining sponsorship from a local restaurant or business, tap the main office or headquarters of that chain to land larger sponsorship support. For a brassiere fashion show, ask the main office to design a top for the event, ask the head office to suggest potential models from their staff and/or ask for major sponsorship.

Source: Kristie Quinn, Event Coordinator and Planner, CarePartners Hospice Foundation, Asheville, NC. Phone (828) 277-4815. E-mail: KristieQuinn@aol.com

19. Switch From Prize Option to Raffle Amps Up Purchases

The staff at Providence House (Cleveland, OH) had a great idea to raise a little bit of extra money at their holiday fundraiser: Sell mystery Santa stockings for $20 each, with a high-end piece of jewelry hidden in one of the stockings.

The only glitch? Once the stocking that contained the grand prize was purchased, people lost interest in buying the remaining stockings.

With one little switch, they were able to sell all 300 stockings and net $6,000 in record time.

Now, instead of hiding the prize in one of the stockings, organizers give each person who purchases a stocking a raffle ticket for a chance at winning a pair of diamond earrings. Each stocking also includes an item or certificate valued at $20 or more.

Source: Natalie Leek-Nelson, CEO and President, Providence House, Cleveland, OH. Phone (216) 651-5982. E-mail: natalie@provhouse.org

20. Consider Pairing Up With Professional Event Presenter

Build an event around something people love, and you're sure to have a healthy turnout. Add in a second element people love, and you could potentially double your results.

That's the theory behind Wine, Women & Shoes (Sonoma, CA), says Elaine Honig, founder and president of the company that helps nonprofits host events featuring a walk-around wine and food tasting, sip-n-shop marketplace, live auction and fashion show.

"Nonprofits can net an average of $150,000 from one of our events," says Honig. Organizations pay a flat fee to hold a Wine, Women & Shoes event. Included in the cost is a best practices guide, intellectual property, templates for print materials and forms, wine partners, fashion partners and connections to national sponsors. A volunteer committee runs the event on a local level, with support and guidance from Honig and staff. Since organizations pay a flat fee for licensing, they keep what they net in proceeds. Says Honig, "It's like an event in a shoebox."

Pairing normally unrelated or contrasting elements, such as men and women's shoes, can generate buzz and even draw media attention.

One signature of the events that doesn't come in a box is the Shoe Guys — men from the community who support the individual causes, presenting the shoes on silver trays and explaining the wine pairings to the female guests. Honig says the Shoe Guys are among the most original features of the events and also one of the most powerful tools the local committees have. "There's a lot of leverage based on how you choose who will be Shoe Guys. How will you use that tool to reach your guests?"

For organizations looking to partner with a professional organization for a licensed event, Honig recommends asking these four questions:

1. What has been the licensor's past success in similar markets?
2. What support will you get from the licensor?
3. What value do the licensor's auction lots have?
4. What added value does the licensor's group bring to you that you couldn't leverage on your own?

Honig also recommends asking the licensing group for references and contacting those organizations to see how it was to work with that particular group.

Source: Elaine Honig, Founder and President, Wine, Women & Shoes, Sonoma, CA. Phone (707) 479-2055. E-mail: elaine@winewomenandshoes.com

21. Auction Rule of Thumb

- One guideline suggests you can expect to receive, on average, about one half of the actual value amount of silent auction items. Assuming that's true, you would need about $10,000 worth of donated items to generate $5,000 in bid income.

22. Book-themed Fundraiser Writes a Success Story for Library

An annual themed gala is helping generate major funds while engaging current and potential donors to the St. Louis Public Library Foundation (St. Louis, MO). The gala is part of the fundraising efforts for the foundation's $20 million capital campaign.

Liz Reeves, director of development and communication for the foundation, explains that in order to engage the entire community, the annual events will alternate between formal and casual ticketed events.

In November 2009, they offered a casual party that became a colorful and creative extravaganza called Stranger than Fiction: A Novel Affair. "We wanted the party to have a literary theme," says Reeves, "in order to remind people what we are working toward."

The event was an instant classic, attracting 600 guests at $75 per ticket and netting $100,000, says Reeves. She says that sticking to the event's theme proved invaluable in its success.

To promote participation in costume events, offer guests specific ideas or examples from past years.

Specifically, she says, organizers and participants played up the literary theme by:

✓ **Dressing the part.** Guests and staff were encouraged to come dressed as their favorite literary characters. "People really went all out," says Reeves. "The costume-party feel added a lot to the atmosphere of the evening."

✓ **Spotlighting literary themes.** Five of the library's outer rooms were decorated for five genres of literature: mystery, romance, sci-fi, banned books and children's literature. The themes continued...

- **In the food** — Caterers from five restaurants were invited to present culinary takes on some classic novels: Seafood for sci-fi author's Jules Verne's 40,000 Leagues Under the Sea; Huckleberry Finn Tarts and Lady Godiva Chocolate cupcakes for banned book desserts.

- **In the drink** — A local hotel donated creative drink recipes for the cash bar: "Scarlet Letter Lemonade" and "A Oliver's Martini, with a Twist".

- **In the entertainment** — Thematically appropriate performers were hired for each room: a marionette puppeteer in the children's literature room, an escape artist in the mystery room.

✓ **Featuring a musical interlude** — A full-sized gospel choir filled the historic, high-ceilinged marble room with music. "We wanted to remind people that we have a large collection of sheet music, scores and CDs for checkout," says Reeves.

✓ **Offering a Bookworm's Raffle** — Young volunteers went around selling raffle tickets for a unique literary privilege: to have your name used in a new book by one of several well-known authors.

✓ **Sponsoring a Shh-Silent Auction** — It included signed books, author appearances at your book club and one of 14 sets of customized Build-a-Bear Workshop plush critters, dressed to look like literary characters.

Source: Liz Reeves, Director of Development and Communication, and Mike Ryan, Development Associate, St. Louis Public Library Foundation, St. Louis, MO. Phone (314) 539-0359. E-mail: ereeves@slplfoundation.org or mryan@slplfoundation.org. Website: www.slplfoundation.org

23. Auction Doubles Attraction With Bachelor Dates, Event Packages

An event that began as a former board member's idea has grown from a small gathering to a signature fundraiser for a Florida nonprofit.

In its seventh year, the Bachelor, Baskets and Services Auction to benefit the Community Service Council of West Pasco (New Port Richey, FL) combines the auctioning of dates with local bachelors with service packages to appeal to a wide variety of attendees.

"We have single women (or groups of women or offices) looking to buy a bachelor for themselves or single friends," says Becky Bennett, special events chair. "With the service packages, married and not-single women can come for the show of auctioning off the bachelors and still purchase great service packages. Even men come to this event and bid on service items."

This year, organizers put 13 bachelors and 12 service packages on the auction block. Funds raised go to scholarships for high school seniors, one adult scholarship and other projects the council does to benefit the community.

The bachelors ranged in age from 29 to "50-something" and offered prospective bidders a wide selection of dates, including:

✓ Dinner and a comedy club.

✓ Kayaking, lunch and ice cream.

✓ Double date in a limo to a yacht ride followed by dinner, sunset cruise and dancing.

✓ Drinks at sunset from a balcony followed by a candlelit dinner, moonlit walk at the pier on the gulf, drinks and music at a local club.

The 12 service packages, each with a minimum value of $500, included:

✓ An enchanted evening package featuring a couple's massage.

✓ A personal chef preparing a Couple's Aphrodisiacs Dinner at either the chef's restaurant or the couple's home.

✓ A pig-out and party package featuring a dinner for eight provided by a local barbecue restaurant and four hours of DJ service.

✓ A getaway package packed with a four-hour fishing trip, a round of golf for four at a local country club, two-month membership and 50 percent off group weight-training classes at the YMCA.

Bennett says the 2009 event raised a record $19,250. Bids on bachelors raised more than $4,000; service packages, $3,600; sponsorships, more than $5,900; ticket sales, $2,600; 50/50 raffle and Chinese auction, $2,000; diamond and ruby ring live auction, $410.

Source: Becky Bennett, Special Events Chair, Community Service Council of West Pasco, Hudson, FL. Phone (727) 967-7509. E-mail: bbennetthfpasco@aol.com

At a Glance —

Event Type:	Bachelor & Services Auction
Gross:	$19,250
Costs:	$3,050
Net Income:	$16,200
Volunteers:	40-plus
Planning:	3 months
Attendees:	250
Revenue Sources:	Sponsorships, ticket sales, bachelor and service package auctions, live auction, 50/50 raffle, Chinese auction tickets
Unique Feature:	Offers dual attraction of bidding on dates with bachelors as well as couple and group-oriented outings

Put the auction stage in the middle of the room to give all bidders a good view and equal chance to bid.

24. Could Your Save-the-date Card Have a Double Life

Looking for a way to get more mileage out of your save-the-date card?

Staff with Catholic Social Services of Alaska (Anchorage, AK) breathed a second life into the save-the-date card they send for their Night of Stars Charity Ball.

The card, which has a stated value of $50, doubles as entry into a raffle for two round-trip airline tickets.

Content not available in this edition

The concept creates another revenue stream, as guests who forget or misplace the cards may purchase a replacement card at the event, says Katie Bender, special events manager.

Plus, she says, the card keeps the event — and the agency — on people's minds, as it has value beyond its stated purpose of encouraging people to save the date.

Source: Katie Bender, Special Events Manager, Anchorage, AK. Phone (907) 276-5590.

25. Plan Ahead to Avoid Top 10 Auction Mistakes

To avoid long checkout lines after auctions end, consider staggering table closing times.

Do you have a silent, live or online auction planned as part of your special event? Don't let all your auction preparation time, gift solicitation, organization and packaging go to waste because of simple, avoidable mistakes.

Charity auctioneer Lance Walker, who conducts some 100 fundraising auctions and workshops for charities throughout North America each year, cites the Top 10 mistakes made by event planners:

10. Not having all the auctions in the same room.
9. Poor item display and not using slides or video to spotlight items during the auction.
8. Poor lighting. Brighter is better.
7. Using small bid numbers or not using bid numbers at all.
6. Closing the silent booths before dinner. Keeping them open holds people longer, increases profits and helps keep attendees entertained.
5. Starting the live auction too late or not on time. With 20 items or less, start later than usual.
4. Not enough energetic spotters to catch bids and keep the mood lively.
3. Beginning the live auction after the sit-down dinner is over. People are at their best while eating.
2. An insufficient sound system. Use at least four large speakers on stands in each corner.
1. Not utilizing a dynamic professional fundraising auctioneer. Don't wait until the last minute to line up this key player.

"Many other mistakes can be and are made," Walker contends, "but auctions continue to be a great way to raise consistent revenue and promote good will among constituents."

Source: Lance Walker, Walker Auctions, Germantown, TN. Phone (901) 322-2139.
E-mail: lance@walkerauctions.com. Website: www.walkerbenefitauctions.com

26. Want to Make the Most of Your Silent Auction? Take it Online

Jon Carson, CEO of Bidding for Good (Cambridge, MA), knows how to make silent auctions work with optimum efficacy.

Carson's business hosts online auctions for nonprofits using techniques gleaned from extensive research. "In person," Carson says, "silent auctions just don't work like they should." However, when that auction is moved online, "The same pair of sports tickets that sold in a silent auction for $450 will sell for $600. It's a matter of supply and demand."

Carson explains how the Bidding for Good model works:

✓ **Timing.** According to Carson's associate Deepak Malhotra, assistant professor at Harvard Business School, live auctions are more successful than silent auctions because of competitive arousal. During a live auction, as stakes escalate, so does competitive excitement, making participants more likely to bid, and bid higher. Silent auctions do almost the opposite. Research shows people dislike betting against friends while socializing, and there is no climactic finish at the silent auction's close. "When you're at home viewing an online auction, that competitive arousal comes back," Carson says. "We know that in the last hour and a half of an online auction, bids spike considerably. It allows people to focus and get excited in a way they can't when they're writing on a clipboard in the middle of a crowded room."

✓ **Higher participation.** Auctions that are part of a gala event are only accessible to attendees of that event, who may represent only a fraction of the potential donor pool. Online auctions can reach anyone in the organization's community — and well beyond — at any hour of the day or night.

✓ **Searchable items.** When people are able to find items they want and bypass items they don't, they are more likely to bid.

✓ **Better donations.** Due to the above factors, online auctions reach a broad base of people who are ready and willing to spend. Therefore, online auctions become attractive platforms for companies to donate auction items simply for the advertising opportunity. Free product equals pure profit for your organization.

✓ **Targeted techniques.** An online auction is a controlled environment that can be tailored to bidders' behavior. For instance, studies show people are more likely to respond to bid alerts that appeal to their sense of charity rather than competition — until the auction is almost over. Another example: Research shows women bid on more items than men do, while men bid higher and more competitively than women do. Online auctions can take such factors into account to create better fundraisers.

Consider offering unclaimed or unsold auction items in a post-event online auction.

Source: Jon Carson, CEO, Bidding for Good, Cambridge, MA.
Phone (866) 621-0330.
E-mail: jon@biddingforgood.com.
Website: www.biddingforgood.com

Tips to Seamlessly Add Online Auction To Your Fundraiser

Jon Carson, CEO of Bidding for Good (Cambridge, MA), shares ideas to help you integrate an online auction into your fundraising event:

❑ Close out 50 percent of auction items online, and bring the rest into a live auction at your event to add interest and entice people to attend. For the items you bring in from your online auction, use the last online bid as the opening bid in the room.

❑ Starting the auction online allows you to take absentee bids — bidders will be prompted to list their highest bids, offering them the possibility to win even if they can't attend — giving you the opportunity to make a profit from major donors unable to make your event.

❑ Preview items at your gala. Displaying paintings, jewelry and other works of art at your gala is a great way to decorate your event and create auction buzz.

❑ Let the online auction stand alone. Multiple online auctions in one year can be lucrative, and help your giving community stay constantly connected with your cause.

27. Get Your Special Event Attendees in the Bidding Mood

Give guests as much interaction with items as possible — seeing, holding, trying on — to build a sense of ownership in their minds.

When live auctions are part of your gala fundraiser, you have two major challenges: finding desirable, big-ticket items from donors, and getting your audience in the right bidding mood.

So many variables impact patrons' feelings, such as:

✓ Did they enjoy their dinner and believe it was worth the ticket price?

✓ Is the room well-lit and comfortable?

✓ Are the registration and bidding processes simple to understand and unintimidating for newcomers?

Consider these issues as you begin planning your special event:

- **'Tis the season to be jolly?** Auctions during the end-of-year holiday season can be iffy for several reasons. People may be feeling tapped out financially and emotionally from gift shopping or uneasy about year-end financial reports. At the same time, people may feel especially generous at this heartwarming time of year. Take a look at your area's overall economy and determine if it has affected your supporters for the better.

- **Find a personable auctioneer or celebrity.** A local notable, or one of your most colorful staff or board members, may be a good choice. A team of two can be effective, too, especially if the guests enjoy the chemistry between them.

- **Keep it short and sweet.** By offering fewer, but higher-quality items, participants won't be as likely to be scanning the program to see how far down the list you are, and how many more items are left before they can exit gracefully.

- **Show the audience the goods.** A fur coat or diamond ring are very portable, and a young model can easily stroll through the tables during the bidding to show interested parties the merchandise. Purebred puppies are another auction favorite that should be seen and enjoyed while the auction is taking place.

- **Set the mood for each item.** Have appropriate music or dance to introduce each attraction. A hula dancer for a Hawaiian vacation, a singing cowboy for a trip to the Grand Canyon or a chorus girl for a Las Vegas getaway make the auction seem more like an entertaining show.

- **Advertise the most desirable selections before the event.** When you mail the invitations, design an attractive insert to show guests some of the exciting possibilities: a limited edition work of art, a brand-new, fully loaded vehicle or an exotic piece of gemstone jewelry from a famous store can build anticipation and help guests plan which items most interest them — serious buyers will come prepared, and if they are outbid, they may console themselves with their second choice!

- **Ask popular contributors to act as spotters.** If a guest's friends are milling about keeping track of bids, they may bid more quickly when cajoled and encouraged by someone they like and know well. Good-natured competition, moderated by a friendly third party, can result in record-high donations while a good time is being had by all.

- **Be sure guests can see all merchandise before the event.** Let them sit in cars, try on furs and jewelry, or play with exotic pets before bidding begins, as well as during the auction. Few buyers will offer significant amounts for merchandise they can't (at least partially) evaluate or see a practical use for in their lives.

The level of collective enthusiasm plays a key role in an auction's bidding process. These strategies will help to maximize the liveliness of your crowd and get them active in supporting your efforts through the auction.

28. Draw Valuable Attention to Your Event Auction

To garner valuable attention for your online auction — and especially your organization — think outside the box as you come up with auction items.

Organizers of The Blues Foundation (Memphis, TN) auctioned legendary musician Robert Johnson's "soul" on the foundation's website. Although it only brought in $60, the unique auction item garnered a whole lot of attention for the foundation on music blogs and elsewhere.

Source: www.igetblues.com

29. Fundraising Is in the Bag for Popular Purse Parties

When a woman sees another woman with a great purse, what's the first thing she asks? "Where did you get that?" That's just one reason to host a fundraising event in which great purses and handbags take center stage.

Realizing the current trend of colorful handbags and purses had women talking, officials with Kinship Partners (Brainerd, MN) created a unique event that features one-of-a-kind, celebrity and designer handbags.

In its third season, Purses for Partners raised $10,000 in April 2010 to benefit the Kinship Partners, an organization dedicated to youth mentoring.

This year, the Purses for Partners luncheon featured a luncheon including both silent and live auctions where 156 tickets at $25 each were sold and 155 purses were auctioned. Additionally, two specialty handbags were raffled at the event.

Elise Mink, marketing coordinator, tells more about securing handbags and managing this event:

Giving bid-winners a little more than they expected is a great way to distinguish your fundraiser from competing events.

✓ Event planners work with area businesses throughout the year to secure handbag donations for the event as well as gift certificates and gift items that are included within the handbags.

✓ To secure designer bags, event planners contact design houses throughout the country who give generously to the event. Mary Frances Accessories is a handbag design firm that creates hand-embellished bags and has given generously to Kinship Partners for their handbag event.

✓ Celebrity bags often are solicited from area celebrities. This year's celebrity donations came from local celebrities Jessica Miles and Liz Collin. At a prior event A-list celebrity handbags were included from Meg Ryan and Jennifer Lopez. These handbags were acquired online and included certificates of authenticity.

✓ Themed bags were also available for auction. For example, this year one purse was given a beach theme that included a beach towel, flip flops and a bottle of wine. Another bag was geared to girls and included a girl's purse filled with nail polish, lip gloss and a journal.

✓ Surprise! When a handbag is auctioned off, the purse is delivered to the winning guest and inside they find a surprise gift from a local vendor including items such as jewelry, gift certificates, lotions and more. Bid winners are pleasantly surprised when they open their newly purchased handbag.

For organizations considering introducing trendy handbags to their next fundraiser, Mink advises holding the event near Mother's Day to ensure high attendance of local grandmothers, mothers and daughters. Start early, she says, to secure not only the purses and handbags, but support from area businesses to fill the bags with donated gift certificates, jewelry, perfumes, chocolates and additional perks.

Source: Elise Mink, Marketing Coordinator, Kinship Partners, Brainerd, MN.
Phone (218) 829-4606. E-mail: marketing@kinshippartners.org.
Website: www.kinshippartners.org

30. Give Live Auctions a Theme

Add excitement to your live auction and get people in a bidding mood by giving it a creative, sure-to-please theme.

Need ideas? Base your theme on:

- Some aspect of your agency's mission (e.g., The Acme Middle School Auction to Wire Our Kids [an event that raises money for equipment needed to link the school's computer lab to the Internet]).

- The type of fundraiser you are holding (e.g., St. Patrick's Day event, country western event, run/walk, etc.).

- The types of items being auctioned (e.g., Sports Memorabilia Auction).

- Special characteristics of persons honored at the event (e.g., Annual Alumni Auction).

31. Pump Up Your Silent Auction

Incorporate different levels of auction items to give medium and lower-level donors a chance to win.

Silent auctions are popular and successful ways to raise funds as part of gala events because big-ticket items are often donated, meaning pure profit for your organization.

But too much of a good thing can cause difficulties: more items than buyers, too much traffic around the silent auction display and lower-quality offerings. For a profitable, enjoyable silent auction:

1. **Choose items carefully.** Be discriminating in approaching donors, asking only those likely to give an item that is attractive, useful and desirable to a large cross section of guests. For instance, a generous gift certificate from a popular restaurant good for a year may bring a far better return than a July week in a time-share condo in Vail.

2. **Remember, less is better.** If your event includes a live auction for big-ticket items, keep your silent auction smaller. Thirty to 50 quality items will be enough for guests to have a good look. Group similar items into themed packages.

3. **Enlist your best volunteer buyer.** If one of your volunteers has experience as a gift shop buyer, worked in a retail environment or even owned a specialty store, ask him/her to serve on the silent auction committee for acquisitions and/or display. His/her skills will make your auction area organized, attractive and user-friendly.

4. **Consider the season.** Will guests be shopping for holiday gifts or stretched to the limit after Christmas bills arrive? Keep traditional consumer spending habits in mind and plan your silent auction for peak buying times.

5. **Vary donors from auction to auction.** If your contingency of supporters is consistent about attending your events, they may grow weary of seeing similar items donated by the same contributors. Ask different artists, jewelers, furriers, travel agencies and restaurants each time, unless their donations are always in demand.

6. **Be sure your display area is large, well-lit and easy to negotiate.** This helps avoid congestion, spilled drinks, accidents, and difficulty viewing items. Leave plenty of room for clearly marked bid sheets and for posting auction rules so bidders can easily find all items — especially one that drew them to the event in the first place.

32. Firefighters Give Their All for Charity Auction

A live auction is at the heart of the annual fundraiser for the Idaho Federation of Families for Children's Mental Health (Boise, ID).

But this isn't your typical auction.

Up for bid? Fifteen tuxedo-wearing bachelors.

And these weren't your typical bachelors.

The well-dressed gentlemen up for bid included firefighters from area departments, smoke jumpers and members of hotshot crews, all part of the organization's live auction packages.

"Each fireman is an individual volunteer and not required to participate through his fire department or crew," says Lacey Sinn, development director.

How does she find participants?

"I have always recruited through personal contacts and have then moved to visiting individual fire departments, contacting local fire department chiefs for support," Sinn says. "And now that our event has taken place for three years, I also contact previous bachelors for recruiting suggestions. We have also had individual firemen contact us and offer to volunteer."

Bachelors are paired with an auction package that includes dinner for two and a local activity such as a movie, rock climbing, a magic show or outdoor concert.

For the 2009 event, bachelors and date packages were auctioned for $75 to $800, bringing in a total of $5,250. Bringing in an additional $3,510 were ticket sales — $25 in advance and $30 at the door. Admission included hors d'oeuvres, a hosted bar, professional photos with the bachelors and an after-party with a live band.

If your organization is interested in hosting a bachelor auction, Sinn offers the following suggestions:

- Begin planning early.

- Solicit a well-known emcee. "We were lucky to have a local radio personality who has donated her time to the event as an emcee the last three years," Sinn says. "I would encourage anyone looking to do a similar event to search out someone like that. Not only did it give us a great emcee for our event, but it also gave us a lot of free promotion."

- Hire a professional auctioneer.

- Choose a location that permits outside catering. "If it is at all possible to find a location that will allow you to bring in your own outside catering and alcohol, do it," Sinn says. "It will save you thousands."

At a Glance —	
Event Type:	Bachelor Auction
Gross:	$11,100
Costs:	$2,000
Net Income:	$9,100
Volunteers:	7
Planning:	120 hours beginning six months prior to event
Attendees:	157
Revenue Sources:	Ticket sales, live and silent auctions, cash donations
Unique Feature:	Hosted hors d'oeuvres, beer, wine and professional photographer who takes photos of attendees with bachelors

Content not available in this edition

Source: Lacey Sinn, Development Director, Idaho Federation of Families for Children's Mental Health, Boise, ID. Phone (208) 433-8845. E-mail: lsinn@idahofederation.org

33. Build Auctions on What's Hot

If you have an annual event that includes silent and/or live auctions, pay attention to what's most popular one year and then build on that in subsequent years. Organizers of one college's event, for instance, saw select bottles of wine becoming increasingly popular (and profitable). So they put together what they referred to as a wine cellar — a collection of fine wines — that brought in thousands of dollars.

34. First Year of Online Quilt Auction Successful, Educational

With the proper planning, even first-year events can prove overwhelmingly successful in generating needed funds as well as awareness of a worthy cause.

Staff and supporters of the Ovarian Cancer Awareness Quilt Project at the University of Texas M. D. Anderson Cancer Center (Houston, TX) hosted its first online quilt auction in 2008. In that first year, the online auction of 68 handcrafted quilts raised $11,440 for the Blanton-Davis Ovarian Cancer Research Program.

To promote fundraising efforts, a cancer center employee collaborated with local quilt stores with the goal of hosting an online quilt auction.

According to Pamela Weems, program director for community relations in the Department of Gynecologic Oncology at M. D. Anderson, the creation of quilts for this cause is sentimental, as many quilters have known someone who has lost a battle to ovarian cancer. Many of the quilts feature patterns that emphasize the cause with the use of the teal-colored awareness ribbon associated with ovarian cancer.

When planning specialty auctions, be sure to consult authorities on proper preparation, display and transportation practices.

"Quilters who participate in this project share a love for the artistry of quilting," says Weems. "Many want to honor the memory of someone who battled ovarian cancer by designing a quilt in honor or memory of that person."

Weems shares tips for hosting an online quilt auction:

- **Attend local quilt shows and festivals** to learn how to properly display quilts and to promote your online auction.
- **Promote the event well in advance.** Some in the quilting community do not utilize computers, so mailings and media promotion are key to having a well-advertised event. Approach local media to support your event.
- **Host a booth at local quilt shows and festivals.** Hand out flyers about your needs for the event including requests for quilt blocks and quilt donations. The Ovarian Cancer Awareness Quilt committee at M. D. Anderson prepared save-the-date cards in November 2008 for the October 2009 event.
- **Develop rules and deadlines** for the online auction. Provide these on your website.
- **Plan a community-wide quilting event** called a Sew In where quilters can gather to piece together donated quilt blocks and prepare to assemble quilts. This is also a good time to ask local news media to join you for promotion of the event.
- **Host an onsite viewing** at your organization to allow the public a closer look at the quilts to be auctioned.
- **Create information cards for each quilt.** Cards can list the quilt's title and number, the name of the quilter who created it, how it was stitched (hand or machine) and other details important to the bidder. When posting images online for the auction, include these facts along with the size of the quilt.
- **Determine the value of each quilt.**

Source: Pamela Weems, Program Director for Community Relations in the Department of Gynecologic Oncology at The University of Texas M. D. Anderson Cancer Center, Houston, TX. Phone (713) 792-2765. E-mail: gynonccommunityrelations@mdanderson.org

35. Use a Release Form to Offer Constituent Creations for Auction

If you plan to auction off original artwork as part of your special event, be sure you have the artists' permission to do so. One way to do so is with a written release form.

The mission of Arts in Prison (AiP) of Overland Park, KS, is to facilitate personal growth of local inmates through the fine arts. Inmates learn skills from professional volunteers during 10- to 12-week courses at local correctional facilities.

The organization's annual gala features a silent auction on artwork created by AiP participants and artist volunteers who agree to release their work for the organization's benefit. Selected artwork is also used on posters and invitations.

"Although it is not the purpose of our programs to produce works that can be used to benefit the organization, the release form (below) is a clear statement by the participant about how they wish their piece to be used by the organization, if at all," says Leigh Lynch, AiP associate director. "Participants receive no compensation for allowing us to use their original works or reproductions, and all funds raised go to supporting future programs. The release form documents participants' full understanding and agreement."

Lynch recommends developing an artists' release form that includes:

✓ Name of art donor and his/her intent for use of the gift.

✓ Explicit description of how the art will be used for the benefit of your organization.

✓ Type of artwork contributed.

✓ Validation date of the release.

✓ Signatures of the artist, legal guardian (if applicable) and authorized nonprofit agent.

Source: Leigh Lynch, Associate Director, Arts in Prison, Overland Park, KS.
Phone (913) 403-0229. E-mail: leighl@artsinprison.org. Website: www.artsinprison.org

Commissioning artwork that is relevant to the mission of your organization is a great way to build interst and attract attention.

Content not available in this edition

36. How to Choose an Auctioneer Pro for Your Event

You have decided to hire an auctioneer for a special fundraising event. How do you choose the right professional for the job?

Through research, says Hannes Combest, chief executive officer for the National Auctioneers Association (NAA), Overland Park, KS.

Make sure the persons you are considering for the role of auctioneer have benefit auction experience, Combest says. For a list of NAA auctioneers, log on to www.auctioneer.org and search by your geographic area and the auctioneer's area of specialty, such as benefit and charity.

Combest says it's also important to interview several auctioneers to find the one that will work with your style the best. "Ask them to give you the results of their most recent auctions and what the challenges they faced were. Be sure to check all references that are provided to them and even see if you can see one of their auctions in person."

To tailor the auctioneer to your specific event, Combest says, it may also be helpful to identify what types of organizations the auctioneer has worked with before.

Other considerations when hiring an auctioneer professional can include finding out what types of marketing the auctioneer plans to do for the event, what types of consultation they will give (e.g., whether they will help you identify the kinds of items to be sold) and what kinds of auctions they have experience conducting (e.g., live auctions, online auctions, integrated auctions — using both, silent auctions, etc.).

Other attributes to consider include the professional's licensing or credentials.

"Obviously, we recommend that people hire a NAA member first and foremost," Combest says. "By being a member of their national association, they have made a statement that this is more than just a job to them, it is a profession."

According to Combest, NAA auctioneers may have two designations that could be considered when interviewing auctioneers for your event:

- Benefit Auctioneer Specialist (BAS) — This designation is earned when an individual has attended an intensive three-day class that is focused on conducting benefit or charity auctions. In addition to the course work, individuals must submit a summary of a benefit or charity auction they held and have it accepted by a peer group.

- Certified Auctioneer Institute (CAI) — This designation is earned after an individual has attended a one-week session at the University of Indiana for three years. In addition to the continuing education classes, the person who completes the CAI has submitted various copies of parts of his/her work for review by a peer group.

Auctioneers are required to take ongoing continuing education to keep their designation current.

To find out more about auctioneer professionals, Combest suggests logging on to the National Auctioneers Association's website, www.auctioneers.org, and clicking on the sections titled About and Find an Auctioneer. Those interested in learning more about the history of auctions and the many diverse types of auctions available can contact info@auctioneers.org and ask for a free copy of the Auction Handbook.

Source: Hannes Combest, Chief Executive Officer, National Auctioneers Association, Overland Park, KS. Phone (913) 541-8084. E-mail: info@auctioneers.org. Website: www.auctioneers.org

Amateur or pro? A professional auctioneer can bring experience and wisdom that will boost your next live auction's revenue.

37. Host a Balloon Auction

Have donated items that don't qualify for your major raffle or group well with other items? Use them for a balloon auction at your event.

Write names of these prizes on slips of paper that you place inside balloons. Inflate the balloons and auction off chances to pop one and claim a prize.

38. Unique Food and Drink Pairings Create Party in Guests' Mouths

Get people raving about your food and drink and you've got a successful event on your hands. Just ask Stacy LaCombe-Kraft, coordinator of special events and gifts at Seton Health Foundation (Troy, NY), where amazing food and decadent drinks are the rule for the annual Hopscotch & Slide fundraiser.

"Guests are not just eating and drinking," she says, "they are experiencing. When people attend, we want them to be exposed to new and exciting food and drink partnerships that essentially create a party in your mouth."

To accomplish this, organizers place stations throughout the room that pair a culinary style with a specific beverage type (Hops, Scotch, Martini Slide and wine). For example, says LaCombe-Kraft, "This year Mansion Catering featured Asian delicacies like Japanese dim sum and sesame Thai chicken skewers with the Martini Slide station. The Absolute Berri Acai martinis were served from an ice sculpture with a built-in luge and the station was decorated like an Asian pagoda."

LaCombe-Kraft says the high-energy atmosphere also appeals to the younger professional crowd they seek to target. They achieve this by immediately surrounding guests with elements that appeal to all of the senses. This year that meant guests stepping off elevators at the venue onto a Hollywood-style red carpet complete with a paparazzi-style photo shoot.

LaCombe-Kraft says the event's success still comes down to having an exceptional event planning committee to help you gain momentum. "Hopscotch & Slide would never happen if we didn't have an incredible team of hand-picked individuals who understand the experience we are trying to create as well as the importance of the cause. Our committee members believe in the Seton Health mission and are dedicated to improving the event year after year so that we are constantly out-doing ourselves.

The event has raised more than $360,000 to benefit Seton Health Pediatrics since 2002 and will celebrate its 10th anniversary in 2011.

Source: Stacy LaCombe-Kraft, Coordinator of Special Events and Gifts, Seton Health Foundation, Troy, NY. Phone (518) 268-5604. E-mail: SLacombe@setonhealth.org

---

Unique Pairings Also Boost Silent Auction

Stacy LaCombe-Kraft, coordinator of special events and gifts, Seton Health Foundation (Troy, NY) says their annual Hopscotch & Slide event not only benefits from unique pairings of food and signature drinks, but from strategic pairing of auction items as well.

"We spend weeks packaging items together, rearranging, creating bid sheets and inventing attractive displays," she says. "We also pay attention to feedback from guests and do our best to obtain donations that will enhance the packages and appeal to bidders."

The silent auction, which is a significant part of the fundraising evening, typically has more than 50 items, including big-ticket items such as packages with concert tickets and sports memorabilia.

LaCombe-Kraft says the auction is set up in categories so people can stick to the most appealing items, like date night packages which pair restaurants, hotels and show tickets together. This year's big sellers included a flat screen TV and Rock Band Hero combo package, as well as a trip to see "Wicked" on Broadway and an autographed Mickey Mantle photograph.

39. Two Raffle Ideas

A manager of a community relations health service in Wisconsin offers two ideas to boost raffle ticket sales during your next special event:

✓ **Sell playing cards.** Participants buy a card for $20, tear it in half, keep one half and place the other in a drawing for half the money raised in the card sale. At the 2005 Golf Classic, volunteers sold cards from the Par 3 holes.

✓ **Sell arm's length of tickets.** In addition to selling tickets three for $10 and 10 for $20, volunteers sold an arm's length of tickets for $30, approaching golfers as they arrived from the afternoon of play and throughout the dinner.

40. Dream Vacation Homes Raise Funds for Nonprofits

Vacation Homes for Charity (VH4C) of Lakewood, CO, enables homeowners to put unused time at a vacation home to good use while supporting nonprofits.

Homeowners complete an application at www.vacationhomesforcharity. org, showing the number of nights available at their vacation home and the value placed on that designated time. The donation is matched to the nonprofit or charity the donor designates on the application.

The use of the vacation home is then put up for live auction, raffle or silent auction to generate funds for a nonprofit.

Nonprofits complete charity profiles at www.vacationhomesforcharity.org. Staff from VH4C contact the nonprofit to offer them donation options that meet their criteria.

Michael McFadden, VH4C co-founder, answers questions on the process:

Do any of your constituents have access to vacation resorts or time shares? Approach them for a one-time use of those accomodations as auction items.

How do you reach persons willing to donate time at their vacation homes?

"Our company, The Society of Leisure Enthusiasts, works with owners and managers of luxury vacation rentals promoting the idea of donating to all clients and prospects. Our mantra is 'Do Good with Vacation Homes.' We're also members of Vacation Rental Managers Association and promote VH4C through them. Most owners, managers and resorts like to use our service because we create all the marketing materials and work directly with the charities. Charities like working with us because they can source several vacations with one call."

How many vacation homes were rented in 2009 to raise funds and how much was raised in 2009?

"We participated in 61 events and helped raise $216,000 for charities."

How much was donated directly to charities in 2009?

"Approximately $148,000 went directly to the charities. The remaining amount was used to cover cleaning costs and fees. More than 60 participating nonprofits are listed at the organization's website — all have benefited from the vacation home donation process. In 2010, VH4C expects to double its efforts in fundraising."

Source: Michael McFadden, Co-Founder, Vacation Homes for Charity – The Society of Leisure Enthusiasts, Lakewood, CO. Phone (866) 789-8222. E-mail: mike@thesociety.com. Website: www.vacationhomesforcharity.org

41. Auction a Chance to Spend a Day in Your Shoes

Give your auction winners a hands-on experience by showing them what a day in the life of your organization is really like.

Event planners with Larimer Humane Society (Fort Collins, CO) created a unique auction item in 2006 that lets the winner experience a day at the humane society.

The auction item, entitled "A Day in the Life at the Larimer Humane Society," includes the chance to go on a rehabilitated wild animal release, ride with an animal protection and control officer, and enjoy a private tour of the humane society, which includes lunch with the executive director. The prize also includes personalized humane society gear, such as a thermos, baseball cap, tote bag and day planner.

This auction item was developed by an eight-person event planning committee composed of staff and volunteers.

"We like to offer some live auction items that are experiences you cannot normally participate in," says Cary Rentola, marketing, community outreach and volunteer program manager, noting the winner of the prize has one year to use it.

Rentola says the package was easy to coordinate, as the animal release and animal control departments are both part of the humane society.

"We have an auction chair who touches base with the staff members this package would most affect and the chair takes into consideration their thoughts and work schedules," says Rentola.

The cost of this auction package is minimal, Rentola adds: "The only cost we directly incur is the bill we have for lunch with the executive director. Our executive director will personally give the behind-the-scenes tour, and then she will take our recipient to lunch at a local restaurant."

They modify the package slightly each year to keep it interesting to bidders. In 2008, the society received their highest bid to date for this item, $300.

"The main objective of this package is to offer our supporters an opportunity that few will ever experience," says Rentola. "It is not something that could be bought, but provides a true glimpse into the world of animal welfare and what we do day in and day out for the animals in our community."

The positive feedback received from the winners of this package has gone beyond their expectations, says Rentola: "Our 2007 recipient was so impressed after experiencing the different behind-the-scenes elements that she wrote a testimonial for our auctioneer to read during the live auction this year, explaining to all of our guests what a unique and educational experience she had. This package is a natural fit for our organization to offer, but it's difficult to fully explain all that the recipient could potentially experience, as due to the nature of the services we provide no two days are ever the same!"

A day-in-the-life prize package could be modified to suit almost any organization. Consider including experiences that the general public rarely gets a chance to see. For educational institutions this may include sitting in on private rehearsals for musical or theater productions.

Other organizations might consider letting someone shadow key staff members as they plan for an extraordinary event or watch as they participate in a televised interview.

Source: Cary Rentola, Marketing, Community Outreach and Volunteer Program Manager, Larimer Humane Society, Fort Collins, CO. Phone (970) 226-3647. E-mail: cary@larimerhumane.org

To stimulate even more bids, ask local celebrities to offer a day in their job as an auction item.

42. Beat-the-clock Raffle

Arrange for a donated prize such as a weekend trip or spa package. Get a windup clock and sell tickets to guess what time the clock will stop. The one closest to that time wins.

Let everyone know when the clock was started and place it in a location that can be readily seen. In case of a tie, have duplicate prizes available or draw for a winner.

43. Ask Sponsors to Help With Raffle Prizes

Ease the burden of trying to get your raffle prizes donated by asking businesses to sponsor big-ticket items. Many places that sell these items most likely have been tapped for donations. Use the business relationships you or your board members have to ask them to donate the item instead. You can recognize the business on the event's program or print their name on the raffle ticket.

44. Raffle Proves Recession-proof for Fundraising

Don't be shy about experiementing with multiple raffles in the same year.

While creativity is a good thing, sometimes sticking with a proven event is better.

A prime example of this is the raffle. During a recession, a raffle accomplishes many things that bigger fundraisers usually can't. For instance, because people can get involved in a raffle for a relatively low cost, it can be a great way to attract first-time donors and increase your database.

Raffles also have staying power and can be held again and again, since for each one, the donor is not being asked to give much money or donate any time. People also like the nostalgic feel of raffles, especially during tough times. And from the perspective of development staff, raffles are practically free and very easy to operate.

The Appalachia Mission of Hope (McKee, KY), a Christian charitable organization, holds 12 or more successful raffles throughout the year. Even though the organization is located in an impoverished area, organizers say the raffles are a hit because ticket prices are set at only $1 per ticket, and because the prizes are always useful and enjoyable.

Ann Williams, director of operations, schedules raffles with holidays year-round, when people are more willing to spend a little extra in the hopes of having something nice for the holidays in return.

"In November, we raffle a huge basket of food items and a gift certificate for a turkey or a Thanksgiving meal," Williams says. "For Easter, we raffle a basket stuffed with toys and goodies for a child. For Mother's Day and Father's Day, we raffle a basket of items for a lady and a basket of items for a man. In summer, we raffle a two-night stay at a motel coupled with tickets to some type of entertainment. We live some two-and-a-half hours from resort areas like Pigeon Forge and Gatlinburg, TN, so these locales work well for us."

Even without holiday themes, the mission has ongoing success raffling off dinner-and-a-movie packages. For a recent raffle, Williams collected gift certificates from seven restaurants and packaged them together into one raffle she called Food for a Week.

One more mission-friendly aspect of raffles is that they are an easy way to foster one-on-one relationships within the community. Williams prefers to sell raffle tickets at the mission's small thrift store, where volunteers can make face-to-face contact with members of the community.

Source: Ann Williams, Director of Operations, Appalachia Mission of Hope, McKee, KY. Phone (606) 965-2449. E-mail: awilliams@amohonline.org

Whether it's getting high-priced items donated, encouraging higher bids or making your silent auction more fun, these tips will help make your next silent auction shout!

Encourage Higher Bids

- Create competition among guests to get higher bids. Before the bidding ends, have staff go around to bidding tables with radios and dry erase boards to solicit more bids. Once they get the bid, have them write the new amount on the board and radio it to staff members. The guests at the other tables will see and hear the bids going up, prompting them to place a higher bid.
- Establish buy-in from your president or CEO to get your audience interested and to raise bids. Ask your executive to give the audience updates on bidding, especially items that have evoked a lot of interest.
- Set a goal amount for each item and aim for those goals. You can concentrate your motivation techniques on those high-priced items to get the most out of your auction.

Package Items

- When packaging auction items together, make it worth the bidder's time. For example, when putting together a travel package, include a restaurant gift certificate, hotel accommodations and a fun activity (e.g., a mini cruise or a ball game).
- Be careful when packaging items together so you don't lessen the value of another item. Be aware of which items can bring in a higher bid on their own (e.g., autographed sports memorabilia).

Get Valuable Items Donated

- Trade services with vendors to get high-priced auction items. Offer them yearly memberships, passes to behind-the-scenes exclusive tours or comp tickets to special events.
- Use your connections to get high-priced auction items donated. Maybe a board member knows someone who would donate the use of a condo in Hawaii or a yacht.
- Utilize the stores you already visit. If you buy your volunteers gifts at a particular jewelry store, ask them to donate an auction piece. You've already made a connection with them and they can write off the donations on their taxes.

Bidding Methods

- Put high-value items on your website and let guests pre-bid on them.
- If bidding is going slow on a particular item, ask your president or CEO to start bidding. Even if they win an item they don't want, they can always donate it back next year.
- Besides including the value or retail price of the auction item and the opening bid, set a required increment level for raising the bid. For example, the next bid on a particular item must go up by $25 or $50. Setting increment levels will help you reach your fund-raising goals.
- Give guests fair warning before bidding closes and watch out for last-minute guests trying to "sneak" in bids.

Prioritize your auction items and focus time and energy on those with the highest potential value.

Continued on Page 32

Continued from Page 31

Make it Fun

- Give your guests instant gratification by announcing the winning bids during the evening's ceremony. That way everyone knows who won which items and they can pay and take the items home that night.
- Ask someone the community recognizes (e.g., a media personality, city leader, local celebrity, etc.) to play up your silent auction. Pick a gregarious person who can motivate your audience to bid and make it fun.
- Make sure your audience knows exactly who will benefit from the proceeds and make it specific. Publicize the cause on all event materials and advertising.
- Look for auction items that correspond with your event's theme.

Popular Items

- NASCAR packages
- Trips (including airfare)
- Parties (e.g., tailgating, picnics, boat parties, etc.)
- Jewelry
- Autographed sports memorabilia — whether it's a football, baseball or a jersey, these items get top bids from fans and have the added benefit of being unique items your guests can't find elsewhere. Pro teams make a habit of getting involved with their community and many have donation information on their website, including solicitation guidelines. If they don't, call or e-mail the team's community relations department to get the guidelines before sending a letter. Also, check with your volunteers and board members to see if they have any team connections you can utilize.
- Golf clubs
- Laptop computers
- Digital cameras and video equipment
- Prints from local art galleries
- Spa packages

Publicize Your Auction for Free

- Ask the event committee members, especially if they're volunteers, to send e-mail invites to their friends and co-workers. Either scan your invitation or create an e-mail invite from scratch for your committee members.
- Utilize free community calendars, your local TV station's community calendars, nonprofit event pages and free weekend newspapers.
- Create signage for committee members and volunteers to post at their workplace.

Solicit Donations

- A great tip for soliciting donations — your neighbors. Solicit other businesses in your building or on your street. You have a greater chance of having them recognize your organization's name or mission.
- Try to follow up solicitation letters with face-to-face interviews. You'll not only make a connection, but it's harder to say "no" to someone in person.

Get Auction Items Noticed

- Put your silent auction tables where guests can't miss them — by the door. Arrange them in a pattern (e.g., a half circle) so they stand out from the rest of your tables.
- If you're giving away a stay in a condo, summerhouse or timeshare, include pictures so guests can see the locations.
- Sometimes people don't like to be the first to bid, so ask volunteers to break the ice by placing the first bid.

Encourage volunteers to think outside the box about ways they can publicize upcoming auctions.

46. Free Auction Planning Calendar

Before planning your next live, silent or online auction, get organized with a 12-month auction planner from www.auctionpay.com.

The free online service offers a detailed planning calendar to help nonprofits achieve their event goals. In the year leading up to the event, Auction Planner can suggest tasks and ideas to help improve the fundraiser.

To receive the planner, visit www.auctionpay.com. Under featured resources click Download the auction planner. The link will direct you to a contact information page. After the required fields are complete, the auction planner will be delivered to your inbox.

47. Add Golf Ball Drop Raffle to Next Golfing Event

To add both fun and revenue to your golfing event, incorporate a golf ball drop raffle. Sell numbered raffle chances based on the winner being the closest to the target's center in a drop of numbered golf balls. To make the drop an attention grabber, use a tethered hot air balloon suspended above a huge bull's-eye target painted on a field or drop the golf balls from a helicopter as it hovers above the target.

48. Tips for Orchestrating the Best Silent Auction

Silent auctions are a tried-and-true method of bringing necessary funds into nonprofit organizations. But success doesn't just happen. To gain the most positive publicity and proceeds from your next silent auction, try the following tips for success:

More silent auction items don't necessarily translate into larger profits, since there will be less opportunity to increase bids in the alloted time. Let your crowd size and available time determine the optimal number of items.

- **Spotlight your main items.** Using well-placed lighting can help emphasize your big-ticket items at your silent auction. Use picture lights, spotlights or fine art lighting to emphasize and feature your main items to draw the bidders to that item. Ask a local museum or curator for advice and tips.

- **Prominently place silent auction items.** Be sure to put silent auction items near a high traffic area to get the most exposure to bidding guests such as near the ticket booth, refreshment area or even the bathrooms.

- **Style clothing.** If your silent auction includes clothing, use mannequins to display these items. Add accessories such as hats, purses and jewelry to complete the look and include them with the auction items.

- **Create and share detailed descriptions.** Ask the writer among your volunteers to come up with well-written and detailed descriptions for the items.

- **Think location, location, location.** Place the most valuable items in the most prominent areas with the most foot traffic to generate the most buzz and, ultimately, bidding.

- **Create and circulate silent auction announcements.** It's important that the event host for the evening announces when silent auction items are up for bid and should offer guests a countdown until close of that item. Allow ample time for guests to make their way to the bid sheet in order to maximize the number of bidders. Announce the close of the item and have someone on hand to pull the bid sheet.

49. Online Sports Auction Beats Event Planning for University

When it comes to raising funds, online auctions are hard to beat, says Whitey Rigsby, director, The V Club, Villanova University (Villanova, PA).

Through online auctions, "We've raised between $80,000 and $100,000 every year for the last five years, without the overhead or work involved with a large-scale event," Rigsby says. In fact, he says, for the first five years of the auction, responsibilities were so manageable that he and his secretary easily handled all of the necessary work.

Five Steps to a Successful Online Auction

The 10-year-old online auction for V Club of Villanova University (Villanova, PA) has a strong history of success, raising $80,000 to $100,000 each of the last five years. Whitey Rigsby, V Club director, shares some of what he and his colleagues have learned over the last 10 years to help make your online auction successful.

1. **Find the right company.** It may take a few tries before you find the best match for you. Rigsby says they worked with two or three other companies before finding their best partner in Sound Enterprises.

2. **Network, network, network.** This is the key to one-of-a-kind auction items and repeat donations.

3. **Timing is everything.** Plan your event at a time when you can piggyback on hype or tie in to other events. The V Club auction runs between Thanksgiving and Christmas, at the start of the men's basketball season. Fans are pumped up about the new season and people are looking for Christmas gifts.

4. **Get specific.** For vacation home and timeshare items, clarify with the donor when the winner can use the prize. Make sure those dates are listed on the auction site along with any supporting documentation. When notifying the winner, make sure to reiterate the dates the prize is available for use.

5. **Do it all at once.** Rigsby says some organizations have open-ended auctions, consistently offering one or two items all year long. "Limiting it to a certain time period allows momentum to build and creates a following. People can count on when the auction is going to be, and they start to look forward to it."

The auction features sports memorabilia, vacation packages and once-in-a-lifetime opportunities, including the chance to travel with the men's basketball team to Louisville or be a Villanova Wildcat Ball Boy or Girl at a men's basketball game.

The three-week auction begins at the start of basketball season, right before Christmas. V Club officials guarantee all items will arrive by Christmas, which Rigsby says adds interest as people are able to bid on gifts for fans and alumni alike.

Villanova's sports teams are able to gain additional benefit from the auction by providing items of their own, with the net proceeds from these items going to their respective programs. For example, Rigsby says, the baseball team raised $30,000 for its program that way during the last auction.

Rigsby works with sports technology company Sound Enterprises (Norcross, GA), which handles the online aspect of the auction. The V Club pays Sound Enterprises 10 percent of auction proceeds and a 4-percent credit card fee, leaving 86 percent of funds raised to go directly to help support athletes and sports programs.

Like any auction, Rigsby says, the event is not without stress as organizers wonder what the results will be and whether all the work will be worth it. But after 10 years, he says, "We're at a point where we have resolved a lot of the issues and securing items is really more of a renewal process now than cold calling. Plus, we have a lot wider reach online than we would ever have at an event."

Source: Whitey Rigsby, Director, The V Club, Villanova University, Villanova, PA. Phone (610) 519-5505.
E-mail: whitey.rigsby@villanova.edu

Online Auction Companies Can Boost Success

A number of companies are devoted to helping nonprofits succeed at online auctions. Here are a few to check out as you search for the best match for your organization:

- Sound Enterprises — www.soundenterprises.net
- Bidding for Good — www.biddingforgood.com
- Idonatetocharity.org — www.idonatetocharity.org
- Charityfolks.com — www.charityfolks.com
- Charitybuzz — www.charitybuzz.com

50. Raffle Entices Captive Group

Sometimes it pays to take advantage of a large — and captive — audience.

Officials at one university raffled away $10,000 at their annual Homecoming event, raising as much as $53,000 on $100 raffle tickets. And on two separate occasions, the winners have donated the entire prize back to the university's scholarship fund.

51. Career Day Auction Packages Grab Interest, Offer Experience

Looking for a novel item to offer at live or silent auctions? Consider a day shadowing supporters with interesting or unusual jobs.

"We offer students the chance to spend a day with an executive from companies like MTV2, the New York Times, College Sports TV, and a local restaurant," Ginny Poleman, president of the Mamaroneck Schools Foundation (Mamaroneck, NY), says of the foundation's Career Day auction packages. "It's a very experiential opportunity."

While the packages are usually used by students, Poleman suggests promoting such experience-based items to parents, who may be more immediately intrigued by the idea.

Source: Ginny Poleman, President, Mamaroneck Schools Foundation, Larchmont, NY. Phone (914) 698-9079. E-mail: Ginnypoleman@me.com

52. Prepare a List of Auction Items

Next time you're planning a special event, turn to a checklist of hoped-for auction items, many of which are unique. You might choose to share the list with select individuals on your mailing list, asking them to help you secure donated items or services.

Here are ideas to help you get started:

- ☐ Free medical, eye or dental exam.
- ☐ Freshly baked pie each month for a year.
- ☐ One-half day of computer instruction.
- ☐ Three-month fitness center membership.
- ☐ Eight hours of free babysitting.
- ☐ Round trip for four on a corporate jet.
- ☐ Cellphone and free calling time.
- ☐ Free advertising in a newspaper.
- ☐ Two free weeks of house sitting.
- ☐ Paid-up life insurance.
- ☐ A designer bird house.
- ☐ Introduction to a celebrity friend.
- ☐ A side of beef or pork.
- ☐ One free year of cable television.
- ☐ 50 shares of stock.
- ☐ $100 in postage stamps.
- ☐ Two hours of free legal advice.
- ☐ Scholarship to a college/university.
- ☐ Free dessert at five area restaurants.
- ☐ Free space/catering for a reception.
- ☐ Treasured collection or antique.
- ☐ Autographed sports memorabilia.
- ☐ Free monthly housecleaning for six months or a year.
- ☐ Private concert at the location of the winning bidder's choice.
- ☐ Fifty percent off on prepaid funeral arrangements.

Don't be shy about spending money on something you know will catch guests' interest. A $100 sports jersey, for example, may very well bring in $1,000.

53. Volunteer Raffle Musters Funds, Fun and Service

When your budget is tight, rely on the imagination of staff, volunteers and board members to find creative ways to pinch pennies.

Here's a creative fundraiser that involves your volunteers personally: a volunteer raffle.

Round up your most dependable volunteers and have each agree to provide a service of some type — babysitting for an evening or weekend, doing yard work, house painting, basic computer instruction, running errands, just about anything you choose.

Once you decide on services to provide, take photos of each volunteer in action. If the service is house cleaning, for example, show the volunteer decked out with mops and brooms ready to go to work. For Web design, show the person at the keyboard.

Make up posters showing the ready-to-go-to-work crew and print up the tickets.

Expenses are minimal and, with the right volunteers matched to the right projects, everyone should have a good time while raising money for your organization.

54. Health Foundation Tackles Big Goals With Multiple Events

Facing a one-year fundraising target of $1.2 million, staff at the Northern Lights Regional Health Foundation of Fort McMurray, Alberta, Canada, knew that a single fundraiser would not be enough. By hosting three public events throughout the year, however, they were able to raise over $625,000 — and cut their challenging goal by more than half.

"Holding multiple fundraisers was definitely a must," says Andrea Tubbs, communications coordinator of the foundation. "Different events appeal to different kinds of sponsors, and attract different kinds of participants. It just creates more opportunities for more people to be involved."

Widely differing in style and theme, the foundation's three main events included:

❑ **Festival of Trees,** a multi-day event showcasing 40 to 50 Christmas trees decorated by various donors. The festival included a snack and gift shop, Santa's workshop for children, and a large silent auction. The one ticketed event — a live auction of all trees on display — drew 700 to 1,000 people and provided a significant portion of the total revenue. Attended by 6,000 to 7,000 people, the 2008 festival raised more than $325,000.

❑ **Spring Fling,** an annual gala event featured a four-course dinner and formal dance. Raffles and silent auctions are held throughout the evening, with a live auction following the meal. Four hundred fifty people attended last year, raising about $150,000.

❑ **RBC Tournament FORE Health,** a two-day golf tournament including a barbecue banquet, live auction and a Calcutta auction (where teams are sold through bidding and earn owners prizes for performance). Additional revenue came from registration fees, sponsorships and the sale of mulligans. The event raised $150,000 last year with 85 contestants participating.

For organizations looking to expand beyond one main fundraiser, Tubbs recommends spacing events as widely as possible throughout the year to preserve both staff resources and donor interest and participation.

Source: Andrea Tubbs, Communications Coordinator, Northern Lights Regional Health Foundation, Fort McMurray, Alberta, Canada. Phone (780) 791-6178. E-mail: Atubbs@nlhr.ca

55. Star-driven Online Auction Draws Big Names, Funds

Project Paper Doll is the brainchild of folks at Monroe Carell Jr. Children's Hospital at Vanderbilt (Nashville, TN). The popular fundraiser engages famous musical artists Kenny Chesney, Carrie Underwood, Christina Aguilera and many more in creating paper doll artwork using common craft-making supplies.

The artists decorate and autograph wooden blocks shaped as two paper dolls holding hands to match the hospital's logo, and the star-studded designs are put up for auction on eBay (www.eBay.com) to raise funds and awareness for the hospital.

Amy Crownover, the hospital's coordinator of eBay programs, answers questions on the successful online event:

MONROE CARELL JR.
Children's Hospital
at Vanderbilt

Content not available in this edition

PROJECT
Paper Doll

Have celebrities help create a buzz for your online auction by creating one-of-kind auction items.

How did you come up with this creative idea?

"The concept of Project Paper Doll came from a brainstorming session between community volunteers Traci and Bryan Frasher and our manager of music industry relations. It was inspired by Traci's vision that local celebrities would be willing to give a small bit of their creativity with an autograph to support Children's Hospital."

How do you connect with stars to create and autograph the paper dolls?

"Bryan Frasher is employed with a major record label and our music industry manager had many connections in the music industry through a former job. Together, they created a Project Paper Doll Committee that included numerous entertainment industry representatives."

How much was raised for this event and how many paper dolls were sold?

"In December 2007, 51 dolls were auctioned, which brought in bids totaling $21,143. In December 2008, 59 dolls were auctioned, which brought in bids totaling $22,273. The auctions were conducted solely online on the eBay platform. The Project Paper Doll series was heavily promoted by the eBay Giving Works Department through a printed catalog and webpage announcements on the eBay site."

This event took place in 2008. Did you have a 2009 Project Paper Doll as well?

"We chose not to have a Project Paper Doll event in the fall of 2009, so we could take some time to examine the program's great success and decide how best to build on it further. I expect the event to return very soon, in a more vibrant way."

What tips do you have for conducting an online auction to garner the most from bidders?

- "Create a unique item that cannot be recreated or purchased anywhere else.
- "Seek a commitment from celebrity participants to announce and promote their involvement to their fans (via their website with a link to their specific auction).
- "Utilize volunteer labor and creative power to the fullest — it creates volunteer ownership and commitment and reduces costs.
- "Seek in-kind corporate support for shipping, Web design, photography, etc., in exchange for on-line acknowledgement.
- "Be strategic in choice of celebrity involvement to maximize outcome — both revenues and exposure."

Source: Amy Crownover, Coordinator of eBay Programs; Laurie E. Holloway, Manager of Public Affairs; Monroe Carell Jr. Children's Hospital at Vanderbilt, Nashville, TN. Phone (615) 322-4747. E-mail: amy.crownover@att.net or laurie.e.holloway@Vanderbilt.edu. Website: www.vanderbiltchildrens.org

56. Change the Rules to Make Your Auction a Success

Gala events with live auctions are a staple of fundraising. But staples can become formulaic and predictable, losing their spark and sapping bidders' enthusiasm.

Sean Kelly, The Charity Auctioneer (San Diego, CA), says that remembering the following things will help your auction come out on top:

✓ **Keep it short.** A live auction should be fun and fast-paced, not something that drags on for an indeterminate length of time. Kelly says an ideal equation would be an auction that features 10 to 15 items and lasts 30 to 45 minutes.

✓ **Know the demographics of your supporters and secure items that will excite and entice them.** Say your audience is a group of mothers between the ages of 28 and 38. A perfect auction offering? A girls' night out with a limousine to the local fire station, where dinner will be prepared for them by the firemen, followed by tickets to a show. "It's important to be this specific," he notes. "I've seen that same group of women sit around with blank looks on their faces when a $15K private yacht bid came up."

✓ **Pass on the items that don't make sense.** Many organizations accept auction items without thinking about how they fit into the big picture. Maybe the items are offered by an important donor, or perhaps the organizers blindly accept anything that's offered. Kelly says auctioning off a skiing trip to a group of older seniors will flop no matter how nice the lodging or the view. He suggests accepting the inappropriate gift only if you can find another use for it (e.g., trading it — with the donor's permission — for a more marketable auction item).

Source: Sean Kelly, The Charity Auctioneer, San Diego, CA. Phone (619) 757-4674. E-mail: funny.sean@gmail.com

57. Alternative to Silent Auction — Chinese Auction Draws in Donors

The luck of the draw brought in thousands of dollars at The Children's Hospital Charity Fashion Show & Luncheon in Fort Myers, Florida. Event organizers tried something new, by putting together a Chinese Auction to raise money for the children's hospital.

So how does it work? Each bidder buys a certain number of tickets for a set price. For example, 25 tickets for $20. Then a box is placed next to each item and bidders can put as many tickets in the box as they would like. At the end of the event, one name is drawn from the box and that person is the winner. "It's more of a game of chance, but the more tickets you buy the better chance you'll win," says Tracy Connelly, the Senior Director of Development for the Children's Hospital of Southwest Florida.

All 520 women who attended the event participated in the Chinese Auction. They bid on 92 different items from dresses, to artwork to weekend getaways. The items were donated from individuals and area merchants. In all, the event raised $50,100 with an estimated $10,000 of that coming from the Chinese Auction.

Connelly says the auction was a success and went better then organizers had expected. "The woman really liked it, they had fun," says Connelly, adding "Many of the prizes were worth more than $300 and if you can buy a ticket for $20 and win, the price point is very reasonable."

Rather than using a silent auction, draw donors in with an unusual Chinese auction.

Sources: Pat Smart, Event Chairperson, Children's Hospital Charity Fashion Show & Luncheon, Fort Myers, FL. Phone (239) 495-8295
Website: www.leememorial.org/childrenhospital/
Tracy A. Connelly, Senior Director of Development, Children's Hospital of Southwest Florida & The Lee Memorial Health System Foundation. Phone (239) 343-6058
E-mail: Tracy.Connelly@LeeMemorial.org

58. Video Technology Can Boost Auction Bids

To boost live auction bids, use video or live stream to show the special amenities of vacation homes or travel sites featured in auction packages.

This technology can also be used to show experience-based items available such as sky diving, hot air balloon rides or cruises giving prospective bidders a better idea of the value of any item that interests them.

Play video on display screens throughout the cocktail hour and during dinner. Then when the item comes up for bid, have the video playing on the large screen as people flash their bid numbers.

Live, streaming video can feature the owner of the time share or vacation home showing off the property, which gives the donor added recognition for the donation and an opportunity to share why he/she supports your organization.

59. Casting for a Cure Offers New Twists for Fishing Tourneys

The loss of loved ones to cancer brought a group of Minnesota residents together to create a new Minnesota-worthy event called Casting for a Cure (Sartell, MN).

Launched in September 2009, the event incorporates the joy of fishing and celebration of life for persons who have experienced cancer within their families. The event's founders are the children of Sandy Karasch, who died in 2008 from cancer.

Joe Schulte, co-chair and Karasch's son-in-law, shares elements that contributed to the first-time event's success:

Specialty items. A commemorative fishing bobber with the event logo was made available on the event website, with 240 selling for $5 each.

PayPal donation options. Using the online money handling system, www.paypal.com, allowed website visitors to contribute. PayPal gifts ranged from $25 to $300.

Digital fishing competition. Participants paid a $30 fee, fished on any lake they wished, then photographed their catch using an official measuring tool and entered the photo.

Maximized exposure on social networking sites. Organizers spread the word about the event and donation options via Facebook and various other social networking sites.

Special sponsor treatment. Sponsors donating $1,000 received a specialty gift basket.

Awards ceremony and silent auction. The awards celebration included a silent auction of fishing-related items which accounted for a large portion of the event's funds.

Funds raised in the first-ever event allowed organizers to donate $15,000 to the Coborn Cancer Center (St. Cloud, MN) and also create a perpetual fund for ongoing events. Plans for the 2010 event called for upgrading pro-fishing level giveaways for the tournament and fostering stronger relationships with sponsors.

Source: Joe Schulte and Tracy Schulte, Co-Chairs, Casting for a Cure-Greater Minnesota Fight for a Cure, Sartell, MN. Phone (320) 250-1010. E-mail: info@castingforacure.org. Website: www.castingforacure.org

> Use technology to allow off-site supporters to take part in fundraising events.

60. Auction Gala Raises More Than $100,000

The Annual Auction Gala of The Covenant School is an 18-year tradition in Charlottesville, VA that regularly raises more than $100,000. Headmaster Emeritus and Director of Advancement Roland Sykes says there is no one formula for building a beloved community event, but he does identify some steps organizers can take to establish a successful auction gala:

Expand your auction — and make it more colorful — by interspersing other forms of entertainment.

- **Take responsibility for the success of bidding.** Live auction items cannot be allowed to sell for too low a price or donors' feelings will be hurt, says Sykes. Organizers must therefore be prepared to bid on floundering items, even if they don't want them. Sykes says he and his wife once bid up and eventually bought a week's stay at a condo in Puerto Vallarta simply because few other bids were made.

- **Focus on entertainment.** Auctions focus on bidding and buying, but the real draw for most attendees is an evening of entertainment, says Sykes. "A good live auctioneer is worth his weight in gold, and a couple lively, outgoing spotters can engage the audience for hours of fun."

- **Establish strong committees and plenty of them.** The Annual Auction Gala is almost entirely parent-run, says Sykes, noting the event relies on six volunteer committees comprised of six to 10 members each. These committees handle everything from acquisitions and food organization to set up/take down and sponsorships and advertising.

- **Involve families of means.** The auction is a great way to get new families involved with the school, and Sykes makes a point of reaching out to those with significant means. "This year we identified six new families who could easily make major donations to the school, and had the chair of the auction invite the wives to help plan the auction. It's a powerful way to help people take ownership in the school."

- **Diversify funding streams.** Revenue generated by the auction gala comes from three relatively even streams, says Sykes. "A third comes from pre-selling sponsorships and advertising, a third comes from a silent auction of 300-plus items and a third from a live auction of 20 to 25 items."

- **Sponsorship, sponsorship, sponsorship.** Of the three main revenue streams, sponsorship has the greatest potential for growth, says Sykes. This area, therefore, receives special attention — the school's 12 board members personally seek and solicit sponsorships.

Source: Ronald Sykes, Director of Advancement, The Covenant School, Charlottesville, VA. Phone (434) 220-7327. E-mail: rsykes@covenantschool.org

At a Glance —	
Event Type:	Auction Gala
Gross:	$104,000
Costs:	$14,000
Net Income:	$90,000
Volunteers:	50
Planning:	6 months
Attendees:	300
Revenue Sources:	Live and silent auctions, ticket sales, corporate sponsorships.
Unique Feature:	With a school enrollment of around 500, the auction involves almost all student families.

61. Fundraising Auction Puts Members' Talents Up for Bid

Consider showcasing the talents of your members in a creative way: Ask them to offer gift certificates related to those talents in gift baskets for your next fundraising auction.

Services and experiences will appeal to some participants more than items and objects — be sure to offer a mix of both.

This worked well for the February 2010 fundraiser for the Northfield Union of Youth (Northfield, MN) called I Heart NuY Fundraiser. The group's 900 members — all between the ages of 12 and 20 — worked to create a Valentine-themed event complete with a pre-Valentine's Day dance party, photo booth, pink cotton candy sales and more.

One key ingredient to the evening's festivities was the auction of donated gift baskets created by members that showcased member talents (e.g., dance lessons, bead-making lessons or home-cooked meals). The gift baskets were auctioned off during the event and proceeds went to the final bidder.

Source: Amy Merritt, Northfield Union of Youth, Northfield, MN. Phone (507) 663-0715. E-mail: northfieldunionofyouth@gmail.com. Website: www.unionofyouth.org

62. Successful Auction Strategies

With 17 years as a licensed auctioneer and a nonprofit client list that includes Make-A-Wish Foundation, the American Heart Association and more major names, Dawn Rose-Sohnly knows what it takes to make a nonprofit fundraising auction a success.

President and owner of Elite Consulting LLC (Maumee, OH), she shares some of her best advice for auction success:

❑ **Establish a contract and understand the legalities related to the event.** The contract should outline responsibilities of the auctioneer and bid assistants; who is collecting the money raised; whether the auctioneer is licensed and bonded; and who is providing the clerks, cashiers, and any other additional help at the auction. Be aware of your state's auction laws, as well as sales tax and license laws.

❑ **Provide Internet bidding.** If possible, incorporate online bidding during the live auction so online bidders participate in real time.

❑ **Plan ahead how minimum bids will be handled.**

❑ **Hire a professional auctioneer.** An experienced auctioneer knows the bid increment levels, knows how to encourage bidding and knows how to communicate with the audience.

❑ **Understand your audience.** If you're asking for $5,000 for a specific item, know you have someone in the room who will contribute that amount.

❑ **Use bid assistants/bid spotters** to help create excitement, encourage bidding, establish rapport and expedite the sale of items being sold.

❑ **Understand the auction software.** Make sure whoever is working with the software is familiar with it inside and out. If you do not have the auctioneer collect the funds raised, consider hiring a company such as Auction Pay to keep the checkout line moving.

❑ **End with a follow-up meeting.** Do so one week after the auction to discuss aspects that worked well, and those that need more attention.

Source: Dawn Rose-Sohnly, President & Owner, Elite Consulting LLC, Whitehouse, OH. Phone (419) 260-7673. E-mail: dawn@elitebenefitauctions.com. Website: www.elitebenefitauctions.com

63. Everyone Wins at This Raffle

Here's a raffle where everyone wins

1. Get several donated items — some expensive and others less so.
2. Tear your raffle tickets in half — put one part of the ticket on the item and the other part with the matching number into a large bowl.
3. Sell chances to draw a number out of the bowl. Purchasers win the prize matching the ticket stub.

This is a good fundraiser for events that will draw a smaller, known number of people since you obviously can't sell more tickets than available prizes.

64. Boost Results by Combining Live, Silent, Online Auctions

How does the Gambit Auction and Dinner of Canisius High School (Buffalo, NY) raise around $300,000 every year? Its 36-year history helps, but so does offering a variety of auction events, says Colleen Sellick, Gambit program coordinator.

The fundraiser begins months before the night of the event as parents and alumni hold up to a dozen parties to gather the 500 to 600 items auctioned every year. This extended season raises awareness of the auction and allows a wide range of supporters to become involved, says Sellick.

At the event, most gifts are distributed via silent auction. Items with bid sheets attached are displayed in five large groups that are progressively closed as the night proceeds. Larger items are reserved for the final group, and a grand finale offers a last chance at anything still available.

Following the silent auction, a live auction showcases two dozen of the most valuable and unusual gifts. Real-time action helps drive bids higher, says Sellick, and limiting the number of items offered helps retain interest and attention.

Raise awareness and possibly revenue by holding parties to gather donations for your upcoming auction.

A gift website complements the traditional auction catalog as it displays all auction items and sorts them into categories to make navigation easier while allowing development staff to analyze the yield from different kinds of gifts and advise prospective donors accordingly. (Sellick says electronics, sports memorabilia, unique items and vacation homes generally offer great returns for their price.)

The school also began auctioning items directly online this year using the online Web service Maestrosoft (www.maestrosoft.com). So far Sellick has simply sold the items outright, but notes that another option involves using the highest online bid as the starting bid for on-site live or silent auctions.

While the online component is in trial stages, Sellick has already seen benefits. "We have received donations and bids from around the country," she says. "In the future, this will be a great way to reach beyond our immediate community. And for now, just getting the word out about this feature has driven people to the website and increased our direct online donations, which is a great start!"

Source: Colleen Sellick, GAMBIT Coordinator,Canisius High School, Buffalo, NY. Phone (716) 882-0466. E-mail: Sellick@canisiushigh.org

65. Raffle, Live Auction Help Elaborate Costume Party Net $200,000

To describe the Anything Goes fundraiser for TheatreWorks (Palo Alto, CA) as an elaborate costume party is an understatement, as TheatreWorks' scene shop transforms into a room filled with props from previous shows and tables each with a unique theme.

Guests don actual costumes from the theatre's costume shop, and the evening's program follows a theatrical theme, as it is a playbill of sorts.

"It's not your typically black-tie formal event," says Mariel Cano, special events manager. "Everyone gets to wear a costume, and they have the opportunity to support a great cause."

Cano shares highlights of this unique event:

- **Costumes** — Flappers, kings and clergy were just a few of the guests at the seventh annual fundraiser benefiting the nationally acclaimed professional theatre. Prior to the event, guests scheduled a personal fitting with the costume coordinator. On event night, they brought a change of clothes so they could check in costumes at evening's end.

- **Set and decorations** — The theatre's scene shop underwent a major transformation as the production team packed tools away and brought out props and parts of previous sets, creating ambiance for the fundraiser. Additionally, each of the 26 tables had its own theme with a free-form centerpiece. Cano describes the centerpieces as resembling a double helix with prop pieces attached to the base with wires. For instance, the centerpiece representing "Radio Golf" included golf clubs, balls and tees. The "Snapshots" centerpiece featured Polaroid pictures and the "Emma" centerpiece included strawberries, an important theme in the play.

- **Program** — Set up as an actual show playbill, the program featured committee member names under the heading, Directed by. The evening's main events were labeled as scenes, for example, Scene 1 — Cocktails. The Cast and Characters featured the names of donors who purchased tables and tickets.

- **Invitations** — The invitation for the fundraiser featured photos of major donors dressed in costumes posing on the set of an upcoming production.

- **Event highlights** — The evening began at 6 p.m. with a cocktail hour, during which guests mingled and admired each other's costumes. Dinner featured entertainment from a TheatreWorks' production. The evening wrapped up with a dance.

Source: Mariel Cano, Special Events Manager, TheatreWorks, Palo Alto, CA.
Phone (650) 463-7125. E-mail: mariel@theatreworks.org

At a Glance —	
Event Type:	Dinner & dance
Gross:	$265,000
Costs:	$65,000
Net Income:	$200,000
Volunteers:	30
Planning:	One year
Attendees:	250
Revenue Sources:	Ticket and table sales, raffle tickets, live auction and Raise Your Paddle event
Unique Feature:	Guests dress in theatre costumes

Elements Add Up to Help Costume Party Raise $200,000 for Theatre

Anything Goes, a fundraiser for TheatreWorks (Palo Alto, CA) netted $200,000 in 2008. Here's the breakdown:

- **Tickets and tables ($77,000)** — Tables are sold at two levels (celebrity for $5,000; star for $2,750). Principal and supporting cast tickets sold for $500 and $275 respectively. Guests purchasing a celebrity table or principal ticket received champagne at a priority costume fitting, plus premiere seating.

- **Raffle ($12,500) and live auction ($73,750)** — Raffle tickets sold for $50 each or five for $200 for chance to

win items such as a Palo Alto Staycation. Volunteers selling tickets for a Botox Party for Four donned nurse costumes, while those selling tickets for the Four Seasons Getaway Package wore robes and face cream.

- **Raise Your Paddle ($39,900 with a $40,000 match) and general contributions ($21,000)** — After the live auction, TheatreWorks gave guests a final chance to make a donation. The auctioneer invited guests to raise their paddles at the dollar amount they wanted to give.

66. Try a Raffle to Bolster Pledge Payments

Need a way to reel in outstanding pledge payments? Try a raffle.

One nonprofit had far too many unpaid pledges as it neared the end of a fiscal year, so officials announced a raffle as a way to motivate people to pay up.

They directed an e-mail and a letter to the group that "all pledges paid in full prior to June 30 will have their names entered into a drawing for a free moped — a great prize for anyone wanting to cut down on gas!"

The result: A whopping 85 percent of outstanding pledges were paid in full within 60 days.

67. Boost Auction Inventory By Sharing List of Meal Possibilities

Planning a live or silent auction? Develop a list of meal ideas for people to choose from and donate as auction packages. Here are ideas to get you started:

- ❑ Tuscan dinner party
- ❑ Prohibition-era speakeasy
- ❑ Kentucky Derby affair
- ❑ Old-fashioned picnic
- ❑ Desserts to die for
- ❑ Chocoholic's paradise
- ❑ Romantic, intimate dinner
- ❑ Mexican dinner party
- ❑ Tailgating theme
- ❑ Western-themed BBQ
- ❑ Breakfast at Tiffany's
- ❑ Retro 50's style dinner
- ❑ Hawaiian luau
- ❑ Spanish dinner party with tapas
- ❑ Meal based on a movie
- ❑ Japanese-themed sushi party

68. Gift-gathering Parties a Double Blessing for High School Gala Event

Looking for a way to get a wide variety of auction items without tapping out your resources? Try holding gift-gathering parties. Laura Henry, director of alumni & events, Bishop Machebeuf High School (Denver, CO), says they get more than half their auction items this way, holding several of these events per year. "We create a fun opportunity for our current school families and alumni and their admittance into the event is an auction item to benefit our Spring Gala."

The school holds a Ladies' Spa Day, intended only for women and a poker party for men, in which their admittance is sports memorabilia, tickets or "manly" items, such as tools and oil changes. They also hold a wine-tasting event, where the admittance into the party is a bottle of wine valued at $20 or more. Henry says they use the bottles to create a wine cellar and auction it off during the live auction of the gala event, typically garnering more than $1,200.

In addition to being a boon for their gala auction, the events boost morale for the school. "Our parents love this program," says Henry. "It is a great opportunity to have social functions off campus all while giving back to the school."

Source: Laura Henry, Director of Alumni & Events, Bishop Machebeuf High School, Denver, CO. Phone (303) 344-0082. E-mail: lhenry@machebeuf.org.

69. Super Charge Your Silent Auction With Roving Reporters

Silent auctions can raise significant revenue, yet sometimes suffer from a lack of attention or interest. Jean Block, president of Jean Block Consulting Inc., (Albuquerque, NM) says such malaise can be counteracted by roving reporters.

"Roving reporters can be staff members or local celebrities, but it's important they have the gift of gab," she says. "Basically, you give these people a portable microphone and they go around talking the bids up, saying things like 'Mary Ellen, do you remember that beautiful crystal vase you bid on? Well Bob Jones has now taken it away from you.'"

Reporters augment revenue by motivating bidders and interesting people who would otherwise be uninvolved with the auction, says Block.

Source: Jean Block, President, Jean Block Consulting Inc., Albuquerque, NM.
Phone (505) 899-1520. E-mail: jean@jblockinc.com.Website: www.jblockinc.com

70. Hold Raffle to Fund Volunteer Recognition

Look for creative, crowd-pleasing ways to generate attention and funds for your volunteer program.

At the Steppingstone Museum (Havre de Grace, MD), for example, an annual raffle helps raise money for recognition programs for its 100 regular volunteers who serve the 300 members of the museum.

The recognition programs help keep volunteers motivated and serve as a way to thank them for their service, says Linda Noll, executive director. Volunteers are recognized each quarter with gifts of T-shirts, hats or other small tokens based on the number of hours they've served within that time frame. At the museum's annual dinner and volunteer awards ceremony, volunteers receive awards for hours served that year.

"Museum programs such as school tours and other educational programs, not to mention all special events, would not be possible without our volunteers," Noll says.

The museum holds an annual raffle to cover the expense of their volunteer recognition program. Museum artisans donate a handcrafted item for the raffle so there are at least six raffle prizes available. Raffle tickets are sold to the membership and to the public where approximately 800 tickets are sold at $1 each, raising a total of $800 each year.

Noll recommends tips to host a successful volunteer recognition raffle:

1. Offer raffle items that are truly unique or handcrafted, making them a one-of-a-kind, desirable item to participants.

2. Offer more than one item in the raffle, making the buyer feel they have more opportunity to win.

3. Keep the ticket price no higher than $10 per chance. Keeping the ticket price low allows for easier ticket sales and offers the buyer more opportunities to win.

4. Make the buyer aware that all proceeds fund the volunteer recognition program. This will add value to the raffle's purpose in the mind of the ticket purchaser.

Source: Linda Noll, Executive Director, Steppingstone Museum, Havre de Grace, MD.
Phone (410) 939-2299. E-mail: steppingstonemuseum@msn.com

71. How to Get Raffle Tickets Sold

Your raffle's monetary success hinges upon the number of tickets you can sell. Every year the Alaska Dance Theatre (Anchorage, AK) holds its FUNdraising raffle, their major fundraiser that brings in $15,000 to $18,000 annually by selling 3,000 tickets at $5 each.

The Alaska Dance Theatre is also a dance school with 700 students. Each student, plus board members and faculty, sells tickets, making it an organization-wide effort.

Ruth Glenn, executive director, says the biggest motivator is creating buy-in with the sellers. Glenn gives a pitch to each class, stressing the importance of raising money and how it will help the school, which makes students feel like they're contributing.

Source: Ruth Glenn, Executive Director, Alaska Dance Theatre, Anchorage, AK. Phone (907) 277-9591. E-mail: rglenn@alaskadancetheatre.org

Raffle Ticket Selling Methods

Here are ideas to get large numbers of raffle tickets sold:

1. Motivate sellers by offering a prize to the person/group who sells the most tickets.
2. Ask area businesses to have tickets available for sale. Use the same businesses every year so buyers know where to go.
3. Have tickets available for sale at the businesses that donated items (e.g., travel agencies, car dealerships, restaurants, hotels, electronic stores, etc.).
4. Keep a list of the previous year's buyers and give it to your sellers. You can create tickets where a stub with contact information is kept by your organization.
5. Ask your connected board members, staff and other volunteers to sell tickets.
6. For member-run organizations (e.g., a rotary club), use peer pressure to get members to sell or buy a certain number of tickets. This usually works best with lower-priced tickets.
7. Offer a bulk-price deal on tickets: Buy 10, get one free.
8. Set up volunteer-run booths at county fairs and city festivals.
9. Offer at least one big-ticket item to drive interest and sales.

72. Maximize Auction Mileage

Yearly traditions can build emotional connections and promote long-term support.

Begin an annual tradition.

Next time you're planning that live or silent auction for your special event, be sure to include one item that is up for purchase and then returned at the end of one year for the next auction.

Examples: keys to a second residence donated for a week each year or an engraved champagne glass plus several bottles of bubbly.

Lightning Source UK Ltd.
Milton Keynes UK
UKOW01f0622070813

214990UK00007B/224/P